Nothing Created Everything

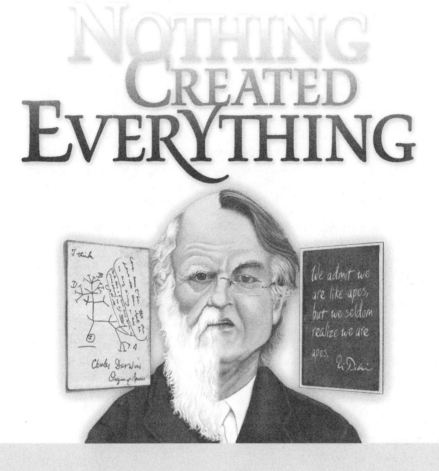

THE SCIENTIFIC IMPOSSIBILITY OF ATHEISTIC EVOLUTION

RAY COMFORT

WND Books

Nothing Created Everything

A WND Books book
Published by WorldNetDaily
Los Angeles, CA
Copyright © 2009 by Ray Comfort

Jacket design and interior layout by Genesis Group (www.genesis-group.net)

Cover illustration by Esly Carrero (www.esly.net)

WND Books are distributed to the trade by:
Midpoint Trade Books
27 West 20th Street, Suite 1102
New York, NY 10011

WND Books are available at special discounts for bulk purchases. WND Books, Inc. also publishes books in electronic formats. For more information call (310) 961-4170 or visit www.wndbooks.com.

First Edition

ISBN 10-Digit: 1935071238
ISBN 13-Digit: 9781935071235
E-Book ISBN 10-Digit: 1935071785
E-Book ISBN 13-Digit: 9781935071785

Library of Congress Control Number: 2009931567

Printed in the United States of America

10 9 8 7 6 5 4 3 2 1

To Richard Dawkins,
in the sincere hope that he looks beyond
the hypocrisy of organized religion
before he goes to meet his Maker

CONTENTS

PREFACE

I HAVE BEEN introduced as "the man who is internationally hated by atheists." We have a love/hate relationship. I love them and many hate or at least deeply dislike me.

One day I decided that I would try and show atheists that my love was more than lip service. I said that my wife and I would pay for dinner vouchers for any atheist that frequented "Atheist Central"[1] (my blog, from which came many of the quotes and questions in this book). Only about a dozen took me up on the offer. One wrote, "You haven't quite converted me yet, but you have shown your true self today and I am forced to think of you a little differently than I did before. Maybe I should stop by here more often in the future." When one said that he would prefer a free copy of *You Can Lead an Atheist to Evidence but You Can't Make Him Think* and a copy of *The Atheist Bible*, a kind couple gave $1,000 for any atheist to have them. Someone else gave $500.

Approximately one hundred and twenty atheists wrote requesting the free deal. I was surprised. The response showed that either they have a need for doorstops or they are interested in spiritual things.

One said, "I love this offer, and I love you and everyone posting here! I really do! Sorry, I'm just bursting with love at the moment! ...I'd love [the book] signed! Hugs and big wet sloppy kisses in a manner completely out of character for an evil sinning atheist like me." Another wrote:

I grew up in a strong Episcopalian household; my family is very devoted—but somewhere over my college years I grew separated from the Lord. I have a few friends who I believe led me in this direction, sadly at this time I would consider myself an atheist—at the same time, though, I feel confused and somewhat torn in two different directions. I am very interested in reading these publications to hopefully shed some light on my situation.

In May of 2009, a pastor in Klamath Falls, Oregon, told me that an angry police officer once said to him, "Pastor! I have a bone to pick with you. I don't get dinner cooked for me on Monday nights because my wife has to be at your church's Bible study by 6:00 p.m." Pastor Jim responded by saying that the man should give him his address, and he would make his dinner for him. Amazingly, the officer showed up at the church the next week with a key to his house, and for the next four months the pastor cooked dinner and stayed to watch "Monday Night Football."

One night they had a disagreement over the answer to a football question. They made a friendly bet as to who was right. If the pastor lost he had to continue to make dinner on Mondays, and if the officer lost, he had to go to church the next Sunday and sit with his wife. The police officer reluctantly agreed, lost the bet, and without telling his wife, put on some nice clothes and showed up on Sunday.

He did that for three months. One night he called the pastor at 11:00 p.m. and asked what he was doing. Pastor Jim said, "I'm sleeping." For some reason the officer wanted the pastor to join him on patrol that night.

After driving around for a while, the officer stopped the car and said, "I want to be a part of this 'born again' thing." The pastor prayed with him and, as the officer prayed, he put his head on the steering wheel and wept in repentance as he yielded his life to Christ. It was the *tangible* love of the pastor that spoke to that man.

So, Mr. Atheist (I say that respectfully), you have a bone to pick with me. You are angry because of the hypocrisy of religion and what you see as blind ignorance on my part when it comes to the issue of evolution. So let's make a bet. If either of us loses we have to agree to forfeit something. So here's my suggestion. If I lose this argument about the existence of God and the promise of Christianity, I will give up going to Heaven. I will give up my life and my very consciousness. You will be right. There's no God and no afterlife. So I will be dead, and I will know nothing. The problem is that I won't even realize that I was wrong and that you were right. That's my side of the bargain.

Here's your side. If I am right and God exists and Christianity is right, then you have to give up going to Hell. You have to be part of the new heaven and the new earth and get a new body that will have no disease, pain, suffering, aging, or death. You will have to enjoy "pleasures forevermore."

I am at a loss, though. I can't show you the tangibility of my love for you. I can't make dinner for you every Monday night, as much as I would like to. But know this. I deeply care about you. My goal with this book isn't to win an argument. It's to win *you*. Yet if I do have a small part in your eternal salvation, the odds are I won't even know about it until we enter eternity. I can wait until then, and hope to meet you then.

Is it a wager?

Yours sincerely,
Ray Comfort

CHAPTER ONE

THE EVOLUTION ILLUSION

I WOULDN'T CONSIDER myself any sort of magician, but I can do some sleight-of-hand. I have seen hundreds of people open their mouths wide in unbelief at what their eyes have just seen. It is true that the eye is easily fooled.

Back in November of 2008 I took a small camera crew to visit the Museum National d'Histoire Naturelle Grand Galerie de L'Evolution in Paris, France. I had a sense of excitement because we were going to be able to film actual "evidence" of evolution.

The museum was magnificent. There were *thousands* of stuffed animals—giant giraffes, massive elephants, zebras, lions, tigers—you name it and you could find it. It was awe-inspiring. But there was a problem. There didn't seem to be anything within the museum having to do with evolution, yet it was called the "Grand Gallery of Evolution."

After an hour of searching all we could find was a copy of *The Origin of Species* in a glass case. So we asked an attendant, who kindly took us up some stairs and showed us an ugly-looking stuffed monkey with "Lucy" written on a small piece of card.

That was it. There was *no* "evidence" of evolution. The museum was filled with God's creation, but all who entered had the wool of evolution pulled over their gullible eyes.

In my home city of Christchurch, New Zealand, the local museum has written in stone across the main entrance: "Lo, these are parts of His ways; but how little a portion is heard of Him" (Job 26:14). You can be sure that these words from the Bible remain only *because* they are written in stone.

VERBAL MAGIC

Neil Geoffrey Turok holds the chair of Mathematical Physics (1967) at Cambridge University. In speaking of the beginning of the universe, he said:

> It is our job as theorists to push those problems to the limit to see whether they can be cured, or whether they will instead prove fatal for the models. Equally, if not more important, is the attempt to test the models observationally, because science is nothing without observational test.[1]

The theory of evolution is scientific only if it can be observably tested. In response to the objection "Evolution is not science because it is not observable or testable," Berkeley University replied:

> Evolution is observable and testable. The misconception here is that science is limited to controlled experiments that are conducted in laboratories by people in white lab coats. Actually, much of science is accomplished by gathering evidence from the real world and inferring how things work. Astronomers cannot hold stars in their hands and geologists cannot go back in time, but in both cases scientists can learn a great deal by using multiple lines of evidence to make

valid and useful inferences about their objects of study. The same is true of the study of the evolutionary history of life on Earth, and as a matter of fact, many mechanisms of evolution are studied through direct experimentation as in more familiar sciences.[2]

Theorists say that testable proof is that "Fossils such as *Archaeopteryx* give us snapshots of organisms as they adapt and change over time." They believe that cold-blooded reptilian dinosaurs evolved into warm-blooded birds. But it is very clear that *Archaeopteryx* is not a dinosaur, it's a bird:

> For many years *Archaeopteryx* has been touted in biology textbooks and museums as the perfect transitional fossil, presumably being precisely intermediate between reptiles and birds. Much has been made over the fact that *Archaeopteryx* had teeth, fingers on its wings, and a long tail—all supposedly proving its reptilian ancestry. While there are no living birds with teeth, other fossilized birds such as *Hesperornis* also had teeth. Some modern birds, such as the ostrich, have fingers on their wings, and the juvenile hoatzin (a South American bird) has well-developed fingers and toes with which it can climb trees.[3]

Another reason they maintain that evolution is observable and testable is because "Studying modern organisms such as elephant seals can reveal specific examples of evolutionary history and bolster concepts of evolution."

One important key in magic is distraction. Here's an example of distraction through an overload of irrelevant information:

> Northern elephant seals have reduced genetic variation probably because of a population bottleneck humans inflicted on them in the 1890s. Hunting reduced their popula-

tion size to as few as twenty individuals at the end of the nineteenth century. Their population has since rebounded to over thirty thousand—but their genes still carry the marks of this bottleneck: they have much less genetic variation than a population of southern elephant seals that was not so intensely hunted.

A founder effect occurs when a new colony is started by a few members of the original population. This small population size means that the colony may have: 1, reduced genetic variation from the original population. 2, a non-random sample of the genes in the original population. For example, the Afrikaner population of Dutch settlers in South Africa is descended mainly from a few colonists. Today, the Afrikaner population has an unusually high frequency of the gene that causes Huntington's disease, because those original Dutch colonists just happened to carry that gene with unusually high frequency. This effect is easy to recognize in genetic diseases, but of course, the frequencies of all sorts of genes are affected by founder events.[4]

Darwinian ape-to-man evolution is therefore observable and testable because they have observed that northern elephant seals carry less genetic variation than a population of southern elephant seals, and the Afrikaner population is susceptible to genetic diseases.

THE EYE

The illusion continues on Berkeley's "one-stop source for information on evolution":[5]

Eyes are clearly incredibly useful, but where did the eye come from? How did so many animals evolve eyes and why do they look so different? This case study answers these questions.

Here you will investigate how eyes evolved and why the eyes of different organisms are similar in some ways but not others. Specifically, you will see how the concept of homology —similarities inherited from a common ancestor—can crop up in surprising places, and how homologies illustrate both the diversity and unity of life."[6]

After showing graphics of the eyes of various animals, they ask:

How are these eyes related? Though the eyes we've seen so far differ in many ways, they all share the ability to sense light. They all have light-sensing cells (called photoreceptor cells) that relay information to the brain or nerve mass—and some of the eyes are laid out in similar ways. But why are they similar?

A single-engine plane has wings. So does a massive four-hundred-seat passenger plane. The only relation between the two is that the makers used similar blueprints.

They say it's because they came from a common ancestor: "Homologies are similar characteristics shared by two different organisms because they were inherited from a common ancestor."

A single-engine plane has wings. So does a massive four-hundred-seat passenger plane. The only relation between the two is that the makers used similar blueprints. Wings have the ability to lift planes, and eyes have the ability to sense light. That's how they work.

The following thoughts about the eye are from a Christian who once believed in the theory of evolution:

We need to revisit (again and again) what Darwin said about eye evolution: "Yet reason tells me, that if numerous gradations from a perfect and complex eye to one very imperfect and simple, each grade being useful to its possessor, can be shown to exist; if further, the eye does vary ever so slightly, and the variations be inherited, which is certainly the case; and if any variation or modification in the organ be ever useful to an animal under changing conditions of life, then the difficulty of believing that a perfect and complex eye could be formed by natural selection, though insuperable by our imagination, can hardly be considered real. How a nerve comes to be sensitive to light, hardly concerns us more than how life itself first originated; but I may remark that several facts make me suspect that any sensitive nerve may be rendered sensitive to light, and likewise to those coarser vibrations of the air which produce sound."

If we like, we can continue to quote the next (and the next) paragraph but his case for evolution just gets weaker. Darwin is using the simplistic method of picking and choosing various eyes from various animals and "demonstrating" gradations of eye development, all the while not showing the fossil evidence which actually and scientifically demonstrates this actually happened. "How a nerve comes to be sensitive to light, hardly concerns us…" "[F]acts make me suspect that any sensitive nerve may be rendered sensitive to light." What? Glossing over something like that is ridiculous. We have light-sensitive nerves (both rods and cones), a lens, focusing muscles, another nerve network to pick up that info, send it to the brain and invert the image, and Darwin explains the general principles of how it all came into being in one (excuse me, two) paragraphs? And that's supposed to be convincing to us? Wow.

Let's be honest—all this really takes faith. A blind leap. I know because I used to believe it myself. Until I started to ask some real questions to my biology professor and he shut me down. Romans 1:25: "They exchanged the truth of God for a lie…"[7]

LET'S MAKE AN EYE

If you lost your sight in one eye, the very best medical science could do is replace it with a fake eye. It may look as good as your other eye, but it certainly won't look as *well*. You would be blind in that eye. This is because we don't know how to create its inter-related system of about forty individual subsystems, including the retina, pupil, iris, cornea, lens, and optic nerve. Nor do we know how to make the retina's 137 million light-sensitive cells that send messages to the brain. The eye is a nightmare of complexity beyond words for those who hope to imitate it.

A special section of the brain called the visual cortex interprets the pulses as color, contrast, depth, etc., which then allows us to see "pictures" of our world. Incredibly, the eye, the optic nerve, and the visual cortex are completely separate and distinct subsystems. Yet together they capture, deliver, and interpret up to 1.5 million pulse messages a *millisecond!*

Russell D. Fernald, professor of biology at Stanford's School of Humanities and Sciences, said:

> At present, we do not know whether eyes arose once or many times, and, in fact, many features of eye evolution are still puzzling. How did eyes evolve? Darwin, the great English naturalist who first brought the systematic explanatory power of evolution to bear on the bewildering biological com-

plexity of our planet, felt that eyes offered a special challenge to evolutionary thinking because they are such "...organs of extreme perfection and complication..." (1859). He was quite explicit on this point, saying "...that the eye...could have been formed by natural selection seems, I freely confess, absurd in the highest possible degree." More than a century later, with new insights that reach from molecular to macroscopic levels of analysis, new mysteries reinforce Darwin's prescient writing. We still have much to learn from the evolution of eyes, both about the existing eyes as well as the processes of evolution that produced them.[8]

He then explained the supposed evolution of the eye:

First was the production of simple eye spots which are found in nearly all the major animal groups and contain a small number of receptors in an open cup of screening pigment. Such detectors cannot play a role in recognizing patterns but are useful for distinguishing light from dark. The second stage in eye evolution is the addition of an optical system that can produce an image.[9]

Kenneth R. Miller, professor of biology at Brown University, added:

Critics might ask what good that first tiny step, perhaps only five percent of an eye, might be. As the saying goes, in the land of the blind the one-eyed man is king. Likewise, in a population with limited ability to sense light, every improvement in vision, no matter how slight, would be favored —and favored dramatically—by natural selection.[10]

How could any sane person believe that the eye simply evolved? Easily. The necessary ingredient to believe is "time." *Massive* amounts of it. *Scientific America* explains:

Time is in fact the hero of the plot. The time with which we have to deal is of the order of two billion years. What we regard as impossible on the basis of human experience is meaningless here. Given so much time, the "impossible" becomes possible, the possible probable, and the probable virtually certain. One has only to wait: time itself performs the miracles.[11]

Richard Dawkins said, "Given sufficient time, the non-random survival of hereditary entities (which occasionally miscopy) will generate complexity, diversity, beauty, and an illusion of design so persuasive that it is almost impossible to distinguish from deliberate intelligent design."[12] Time performs miracles.

Look at how his childlike faith in time causes Professor Miller to abandon all sense of reason:

> Intelligent Design advocates content that evolution could not have produced such complex structures and processes because its instrument, natural selection, simply isn't up to the task. Such advocates agree that natural selection does a splendid job of working on the variation that exists within a species. Given a range of sizes, shapes, and colors, those individuals whose characteristics give them the best chance to reproduce will pass on traits that will increase in frequency in the next generation. The real issue, therefore, is whether or not the "input" into genetic variation, which is often said to be the result of random mutation, can provide the beneficial novelty that would be required to produce new structures, new systems, and even new species. Could the marvelous structures of the eye have been produced "just by chance?"
>
> The simple answer to that question is "no." The extraordinary number of physiological and structural changes that would have to appear at once to make a working, functioning eye is simply too much to leave to chance. The eye could

not have evolved in a single event. That, however, is not the end of the story. The real test is *whether or not the long-term combination of genetic variation and natural selection could indeed produce a structure as complex and well-adapted as the eye*, and the answer to that question is a resounding "yes."[13]

"Long term" (time) performs the impossible miracle for the wide-eyed professor. When Richard Dawkins was asked how an eye could possibly have evolved, he simply said, "Audiences nevertheless appreciate an answer, and I have usually fallen back on the sheer magnitude of geological time."[14] No one was back in time to see the unseen do its impossible work, but those who believe don't need to see. They simply believe.

Scientists have yet to find even a single mutation that increases genetic information. The fact is that there is no evidence showing that mutations have ever created any new features.

Richard Dawkins, in *A Devil's Chaplain* says:

The evolution of the vertebrate eye must have been progressive. Ancient ancestors had a very simple eye, containing only a few features good for seeing. We don't need evidence for this (although it is nice that it is there). *It has to be true because the alternative—an initially complex eye, well-endowed with features good for seeing—pitches us right back to Hoyle country and the sheer cliff of improbability.* There must be a ramp of step-by-step progress towards the modern, multifeatured descendant of that optical prototype.

Of course, in this case, modern analogs of every step up the ramp can be found, working serviceably in dozens of eyes dotted independently around the animal kingdom. But even without these examples, we could be confident that there must have been a gradual, progressive increase in the number of features which an engineer would recognize as contributing towards optical quality. Without stirring from our armchair, we can see that it must be so."[15]

Yet we now know that mutations can only modify or eliminate existing structures, not create new ones. In our genetic blueprint, the DNA letters that define these features can occasionally be rearranged or lost through mutations but will not explain the additions needed by evolution. *Scientists have yet to find even a single mutation that increases genetic information.* The fact is that there is no evidence showing that mutations have ever created any new features.

S. G. Scott doesn't speculate. He says:

> There are no examples of natural inorganic (non-living) materials ever forming themselves into living (organic) material, let alone organizing themselves to the level of being able to duplicate themselves; not to mention developing a system that could store and retrieve the information on how to do it so that their offspring could also duplicate themselves, and could also pass the information on to their offspring, and so on, and so on, and so on...[16]

> ...mutations do not lead to an increase in information. Indeed, reducing the number of legs may alter the body plan, but it does not explain the origin of legs in the first place. Nor does it explain where the genetic information to produce wings came from.[17]

> Successful macro-evolution requires the addition of *new* information and *new* genes that produce *new* organs and systems.[18]

Scientific American, March 2003 issue:

Although evolutionary theory provides a robust explanation for the appearance of minor variations in the size and shape of creatures and their component parts, it does not yet give as much guidance for understanding the *emergence of entirely new structures, including* digits, limbs, *eyes*, and feathers."[19] (italics added)

Still, it's up to you. If you want to continue to believe, you will. Such is human nature.

CHAPTER TWO

THE INTELLECTUAL EMBARRASSMENT

"I am angry at you Ray. STOP, STOP, STOP saying that an atheist is someone who believes something came out of nothing."[1]

R OBERT MADEWELL (professed atheist) wrote, "Just because a few atheists believe that everything came from nothing doesn't mean that all atheists believe that." However, it's not a matter of not believing it. It's a matter of *definition*. If you say of your Ford Expedition that you have no belief that there was a maker, then you think that nothing made it. It just happened. You have defined yourself as having that mentality.

So if you call yourself an atheist, you are saying that you have no belief in a God—a Creator. Creation just happened. Everything you see—all the different breeds of dog (both male and female), all the different breeds of cat (both male and female), all the different fish in the ocean (both male and female), giraffes, elephants, cattle, sheep, horses, birds, flowers, trees, the sun, the moon, the stars, the four seasons, night and day, the marvels of the human body, the eye with its millions of light sensitive cells

—all these marvels of creation were made by nothing. They all just happened. That's atheism at its core.

Then the professing atheist has the unbelievable gall to consider himself intelligent and he thinks that science backs up his delusion. Think of the ludicrous language an atheist is forced to use. He can't say that creation was "created," and he has to avoid saying that everything has been "made." He will even say that he has no beliefs...that he is "without belief." His problem is that he hasn't thought his beliefs through. If he has any intellectual self-respect he will move from "nothing created everything" to "something created everything but I just don't know what it was." And in doing so he distances himself from the embarrassing label of "atheist."

AN ATHEIST RESPONDS ABOUT NOTHING

There are a gazillion kind of atheists. And each might "believe" differently. The question contains many hidden meanings, and its purpose is to lead to equivocation. "Nothing created anything" would be correct if we re-write it to say: Atheists do not believe that anything was "created." That one would encompass most atheists, I guess. And there is no embarrassment for that. Nor intellectual, nor otherwise. But it is incorrect if it means: Atheists believe that "nothing" was the "creative force" that produced the universe. Not because it "would be an intellectual embarrassment," but because that does not describe what any atheist I know thinks (not believes, but thinks). I bet most would claim not to know what if anything produced the universe. We could cite big bangs and such, but &!$*, I do not understand anything of those theories. But that does not mean God, nor that "nothingness" would be something I "believe" to be a creative force. So, what do I think (not believe, think), well, I think that natural processes are behind the universe. Not "nothing" but natural processes. It would be more accurate if Ray said, "Atheists believe that nobody created the universe."

Look at the sad and embarrassing intellectual hoops this man has had to go through to keep God out of his beliefs. Like the typical atheist, he thinks that nothing was "created," that we are not living in a "creation"—because that has strong connotations of there being a Creator. He therefore can't use the word "made," because that speaks of a Maker—and that speaks of God, and any thoughts of God speaks of some sort of moral responsibility.

So he is saying that material (creation) exists, but there was no force that brought it into being. He thinks that nothing brought it into being. So we (once again) have a clear definition of an atheist. An atheist is someone who thinks (but doesn't believe) that nothing created everything.

There's no way to say it kindly, but such thoughts show that the atheist doesn't think, and prove the Bible right when it says that the fool has said in his heart that there is no God (see Psalm 14:1 and Romans 1:20).

He concludes by saying, "It would be more accurate if Ray said, 'Atheists believe that nobody created the universe.'" Let me change one word to make what he is saying make more sense: "It would be more *comfortable* if Ray said, 'Atheists believe that nobody created the universe.'"

ANOTHER ATHEIST RESPONDS

It's not the "nothing" we have a problem with, it's the "created" and you've heard this a million times you creepy ignorant man. If you ask me: "What created the universe?" I will answer "Nothing." You will then proudly quote me as holding the position that "Nothing created everything"...

and for this I have every reason to call you a stinking liar, because what I actually believe is that the universe was not "created" in the first place. Just like you believe your insubstantial God was not "created."

Those who believe that the universe is eternal (that it wasn't created) reveal their lack of understanding of basic science. Look at the words of Stephen Hawking: "The conclusion of this lecture is that the universe has not existed forever. Rather, the universe, and time itself, had a beginning in the Big Bang, about 15 billion years ago" (The Beginning of Time).

There is disagreement about how long ago the universe began, but there is no doubt among scientists that it had a beginning. So the belief that it wasn't created is completely unfounded. Which brings each of us back to the question: "What was the initial cause?" That Cause was God.

So where is God? The Bible tells us that we are in His presence. No matter where you go, no matter what you do, you are seen by the God who requires an account of every thought, word, and deed. It is your God-given right not to believe that, but you will only deny it to your own eternal detriment. God offers you complete forgiveness of sins and the gift of everlasting life (see Romans 6:23). If you refuse, then you will have no one to blame but yourself. On that Day you will realize that in that respect I wasn't a creepy ignorant man, and that I wasn't a stinking liar, but told you the truth. And I did so because I care about you and where you spend eternity.

God has no beginning or end. He is eternal. That's why (when Moses asked for His name) He simply said "I AM" (see Exodus 3:14). God just "is."

Without the grace of God all of us, including the atheist, have as much understanding of the subject of God as a dead chicken has of the theory of relativity. Our understanding is "darkened."

We are alienated from the life of God through the ignorance that is in us because of the blindness of our heart (see Ephesians 4:18). Look closely at the next verse (Ephesians 4:19) to see the root of our problem:

> [H]aving their understanding darkened, being alienated from the life of God, because of the ignorance that is in them, because of the blindness of their heart; who, being past feeling, have given themselves over to lewdness, to work all uncleanness with greediness. (Lewd: "inclined to, characterized by, or inciting to lust or lechery; lascivious.")

However, in reference to His eternality, God created the dimension of time to which He then subjected humanity. When you and I die we will leave time and go into eternity. To think of such a dimension strains the mind. But use the brain for a moment to think of the infinitude of space. It has neither beginning nor end, despite the simple surmising of some who believe that space has an end. It goes on forever in every direction...and Almighty God *fills* the entirety of space.

This same incredible Creator is morally perfect and demands perfect justice. So please make sure you have peace with Him when you stand before Him on the Day of Judgment. On that Day, the dumbest of Christians will be seen to be ten thousand times wiser than the wisest of atheists.

I guess that a high-profile Brooklyn-based atheist didn't think too deeply about the title of her new book. It's a double whammy, called *Nothing: Something to Believe in*. The title reveals the two best kept secrets of atheism. 1. An atheist *does* have a belief. 2. He believes that nothing created everything.

If you choose to be called an "atheist," that's the intellectually embarrassing cross you have to carry, but you carry it by your own choice.

For many years I have appealed to the logic of everything material necessitating a Creator. When I have done this, I have noticed that atheists run to a predictable refuge. See if you can see how they deal with it:

"If some sort of evidence turned up that a conscious entity was behind the creation of the universe itself…then it would simply open up this huge question of what this entity is and where it came from."

"So Ray, what is the explanation of where God came from?"

"If everything needs a maker, who made the maker?"

Whatever created everything, it had to be nonmaterial (unseen), eternal (without beginning or end), and omnipotent (having the amazing ability to create everything from nothing).

"Alright, I'll bite. Okay, a creator created the Universe. Where did this creator come from?"

It is scientifically impossible for nothing to create everything. If nothing created everything, then the "nothing" isn't nothing. It is something, because it had the amazing ability to create everything. Only an unscientific ignoramus would hold to the thought that nothing created everything. We have the dilemma of having everything, so we therefore have to come to the conclusion that something made it. Whatever it was, it had to be nonmaterial (unseen), eternal (without beginning or end), and omnipotent (having the amazing ability to create everything from nothing). If the professing atheist concedes to such basic logic (which he must or he reveals that he is unscientific and unintelligent), then he's not an atheist. He is in truth an agnostic ("one who is skeptical about the existence of God but does not profess true atheism."). He is someone who believes that there was a creative force that brought everything into existence, but for some reason he denies that it was God.

Here's the complete e-mail from the angry atheist who wants me to stop:

> I am angry at you Ray. STOP, STOP, STOP saying that an atheist is someone who believe something came out of nothing. I am an atheist and this is what I believe. Matter and energy cannot be created or destroyed however they can change from one form to another. This is known as the first law of thermodynamics. Therefore it is natural to believe that matter or energy has always existed in one form. This is why we get upset when you tell us that we believe something came out of nothing. Because there has never been nothing; matter or energy has always existed."

A CHALLENGE TO A PROFESSOR

P. Z. Myers, a biologist and associate professor at the University of Minnesota, was a little upset by my definition of what an atheist believes. The statement is a huge dilemma for the professor, because he knows that only a fool could believe the scientific impossibility that nothing created everything. He can't say that the universe is eternal, because he knows that it's not. So he is left with the predicament of having to admit that *something* created everything. Professor Myers believes in a Creator of some sort; he just doesn't know its identity. He may be a professor of atheism, but he is in truth just an agnostic. So he defaults to the predictable "Well, who made God then?" This is what he said: "And of course, he doesn't bother with this problem: who made God? I can guess how he'd respond: there was no 'who,' and God wasn't 'made.' At which time we do a little judo move and point out that the universe wasn't 'made' by a 'who,' either."

Here now is a big mystery. He doesn't know how the universe got here, but he somehow knows that the Creator wasn't a "who." How does he know that? Does he have some inside information? I would like to hear it. How does he know that a "who" wasn't involved in creation? Even Richard Dawkins knows better. He's a little more careful with his wording, with his "Why There Almost Certainly is no God."[2]

If you are familiar with the first law of thermodynamics, then you should be familiar with the second law. It tells us that it is scientifically impossible for the universe to be eternal. Everything degenerates. Leave an apple on a table for a few weeks and it will rot. Leave a rock for a billion years and it will turn to dust. If the universe were eternal (trillions and trillions-plus years old) it would have turned to dust. So now you are back to the question of what caused the universe in the beginning. If you say that there was no first cause (a Creator), then you are stuck with the unscientific and thoughtless belief that nothing created everything. So, what is it that you believe? Is it that something created everything? Then you are not an atheist because you believe in a Creator. Or do you believe that nothing created it? There is no in-between.

Do atheists believe that nothing created everything? See for yourself that this is not some fringe group:

- "It is now becoming clear that everything can—and probably did—come from nothing." —Robert A. J. Matthews, physicist, Ashton University, England

- "Space and time both started at the Big Bang and therefore there was nothing before it." —Cornell University Ask an Astronomer[3]

- "Even if we don't have a precise idea of exactly what took place at the beginning, we can at least see that the origin of the universe from nothing need not be unlawful or unnatural or unscientific." —Paul Davies, physicist, Arizona State University

- "Assuming the universe came from nothing, it is empty to begin with…Only by the constant action of an agent outside the universe, such as God, could a state of nothingness be maintained. The fact that we have something is just what we would expect if there is no God." —Victor J. Stenger, atheist, professor of physics, University of Hawaii. Author of *God: The Failed Hypothesis. How Science Shows That God Does Not Exist*

- "Few people are aware of the fact that many modern physicists claim that things—perhaps even the entire universe—can indeed arise from nothing via natural processes." —"Creation *ex nihilo*—Without God (1997)," atheist, Mark I. Vuletic

- "To understand these facts we have to turn to science. Where did they all come from, and how did they get so darned outrageous? Well, it all started with nothing." —"Fifty Outrageous Animal Facts," Animal Planet[4]

- "To the average person it might seem obvious that nothing can happen in nothing. But to a quantum physicist, nothing is, in fact, something." —*Discover Magazine* "Physics & Math / Cosmology"[5]

- "Some physicists believe our universe was created by colliding with another, but Kaku [a theoretical physicist at City University of New York] says it also may have sprung from nothing…" —Scienceline.org

- "It is rather fantastic to realize that the laws of physics can describe how everything was created in a random quantum fluctuation out of nothing, and how over the course of 15 billion years, matter could organize in such complex ways that we have human beings sitting here, talking, doing things intentionally." —Alan Harvey Guth theoretical physicist and cosmologist, *Discover Magazine*, April 1, 2002

- "If symmetry is perfect on a cosmic scale, the total amount of energy in the universe is actually zero. Does this mean that nothing caused the universe? If our universe is an absolute zero, absolutely nothing seems required to cause it! Is our universe such an ultimate absolute accident? Is it nothing that was caused by nothing for no reason at all? Extreme Big Accident Cosmology answers affirmatively. This cosmology is advocated by Quantum Cosmologists like Edward P. Tryon, Peter Atkins, A. Vilenkin, Victor J. Strenger, Quentin Smith, and a few others for whom the origin of our universe was a stupendous accident, having no cause whatsoever." —R.B. Edwards, *What Caused the Big Bang?* page 163

CARICATURED SOPHISTICATION

R.C. Sproul said:

> Some modern theorists believe that the world was created by nothing. Note the difference between saying that the world was created *from* nothing and saying that the universe was created *by* nothing. In this modern view the rabbit comes out of the hat with no rabbit, a hat, or even a magician. The modern view is far more miraculous that the biblical world view. It suggests that nothing created something. More than that, it holds that nothing created everything—quite a feat

indeed! Now surely there aren't serious people who are running around in this scientific age claiming that the universe was created by nothing, are there? Yes, scores of them. To be sure, they don't say it quite the way I have said it, and they would probably be annoyed with me for stating their views in such a manner. They'd undoubtedly protest that I have given a distorted caricature of their sophisticated position. OK. True—they don't say that the universe was created by nothing; they say that the universe was created by chance. But chance is no thing. It has no weight, no measurements, no power. It is merely a word we use to describe mathematical possibilities. It can do nothing. It can do nothing because it is nothing. To say that the universe was created by chance is to say that it came from nothing. That is intellectual madness.[6]

CHAPTER THREE

HOW DID
LIFE BEGIN?

EVOLUTION TELLS us that life evolved from something. However, the question may be asked where rocks came from. Rocks are not "life." They don't have a brain or a heart, lungs, or blood. Rocks don't reproduce themselves, unless you call breaking in half "reproduction." A rock doesn't fit into the normal definition of life. So where did they come from? The evolutionary explanation is that suns exploded and cooled down over billions of years. Hence, rocks. Ask then where did the suns come from and you will hear that all of them started from a tiny "dot" that is smaller than a period at the end of a sentence. Ask where the dot came from and they will say that they don't know. The origin of life to the Genesisophobic is the big mystery. Still, that doesn't stop them from having ideas. Ask A Scientist answers the question of life's origin this way:

The origin comes from these general ideas:

1) Space origin—meteorites, etc.—we have found amino acids, building molecules of nucleic acids and water in meteorites.

2) Organic soup and the heterotrophic hypothesis—Urey-Miller experiment and the idea that some chemical began to rob energy from other molecules in the hypothetical organic soup. Coacervate experiments back this up by providing an idea of how cells formed.

3) Cairns (and others) Ideas of chemical determination in clay—this is backed up somewhat by finding life in rocks three miles into the crust.

4) There are others. Of course the pseudoscience ideas are always thrown in by religious interests, but of course are not substantiated by scientific investigations.[1]

Notice that any thought that God could be the genesis of life is dismissed as pseudoscience. He doesn't know how life began, but he *does* know that God had nothing to do with it.

When Andrew Knoll, professor of biology at Harvard was asked, "How does life form?" he responded, "The short answer is we don't really know how life originated on this planet. There have been a variety of experiments that tell us some possible roads, but we remain in substantial ignorance."[2]

Time magazine said:

This summer a startling, if still sketchy, synthesis of the new ideas emerged during a weeklong meeting of origin-of-life researchers in Barcelona, Spain. Life, it now appears, did not dawdle at the starting gate, but rushed forth at full gallop. UCLA paleobiologist J. William Schopf reported finding fossilized imprints of a thriving microbial community sandwiched between layers of rock that is 3.5 billion years old. This, along with other evidence, shows that life was well established only a billion years after the earth's formation, a much faster evolution than previously thought. Life did not arise under calm, benign conditions, as once assumed, but under the hellish skies of a planet racked by volcanic eruptions and menaced by comets and asteroids. In fact, the intruders from outer space may have delivered the raw materials necessary for life. So robust were the forces that gave rise to the first living organisms that it is entirely possible, many researchers believe, that life began not once but several times before it finally "took" and colonized the planet.[3]

Perhaps it was *Time* magazine's "intruders from outer space" that provided the seed for Richard Dawkin's believing that some intelligent visiting alien started life. Professor Dawkins said:

> It could come about in the following way: it could be that, at some earlier time *somewhere in the universe a civilization evolved* by probably by some kind of Darwinian means to a very very high level of technology and designed a form of life that they seeded onto perhaps this planet...and that *designer could well be a higher intelligence from elsewhere in the universe.*"[4]

He's not alone with his celestial thoughts: "Chandra Wickramasinghe from Cardiff University, UK, has long argued the case for cometary panspermia, the idea that comets are infected with primitive life forms and delivered life to the early Earth. That would explain why life on Earth arose so quickly after our planet formed around 4.5 billion years ago."[5]

So if comets are responsible for coming to this earth, carrying life forms, where did they come from? Who made them? Why were there life forms on the comets? For the answer, scientists go back to the original dreamer. He had the "conceptual might" to imagine a possible scenario:

> It took the conceptual might of Charles Darwin to imagine a biologically plausible scenario for life's emergence. In an oft quoted letter, written in 1871, Darwin sug-

gested that life arose in a "warm little pond" where a rich brew of organic chemicals, over eons of time, might have given rise to the first simple organisms. For the next century, Darwin's agreeable hypothesis, expanded upon by other theorists, dominated thinking on the subject. Researchers decided that the "pond" was really the ocean and began trying to figure out where the building blocks of life could have come from."[6]

But Darwin's "warm little pond" opens a can of worms. Where did *it* come from, and why was there a "rich brew of organic chemicals" in the pond? It doesn't answer where life came from at all. Besides, scientists now believe that his pond was actually an ocean, which just makes the problem of where it came from larger and deeper.

Darwin's "warm little pond" opens a can of worms. Where did it come from, and why was there a "rich brew of organic chemicals" in the pond? It doesn't answer where life came from at all.

Meanwhile, older and older fossils have all but proved that life did not evolve at the leisurely pace Darwin envisioned. Perhaps most intriguing of all, the discovery of organisms living in oceanic hot springs has provided a Stygian alternative to Darwin's peaceful picture. Life, says microbiologist Karl Stetter of the University of Regensburg in Germany, may not have formed in a nice, warm pond, but in "a hot pressure cooker."

If scientists have, by and large, tossed out the old ideas, they have not yet reached a consensus on the new. The current version of the story of life is a complex tale with many solid facts, many holes and no shortage of competing theories on how to fill in the missing pieces."[7]

In an article entitled "How Did Life Begin? New Research Suggests Meteorites May Have Helped," Joel Kontinen writes:

> Joel Kontinen Level: Platinum:
> My background includes an MA in translation studies and a BA in Bible and Theology. I have written three novels in Finnish, my mother tongue....
> Since Charles Darwin's day, theories about the birth of life have come and gone. Darwin famously speculated about life having begun in a warm pond. Researchers tested the idea in 2006 and found it wanting. They examined hot puddles in Kamchatka, Russia, and Mount Lassen in California and discovered that "hot acidic waters containing clay do not provide the right conditions for chemicals to assemble themselves into 'pioneer organisms.'"
> Stanley Miller and Harold Urey conducted a famous experiment in 1953. While it has been used as a propaganda device for evolution, Jonathan Wells and other Darwin skeptics have pointed out its flaws. Wells said: "The Miller-Urey experiment used a simulated atmosphere that geochemists now agree was incorrect, it was not the 'first successful attempt to show how organic molecules might have been produced on the early Earth.' When conditions are changed to reflect better knowledge of the Earth's early atmosphere, the experiment doesn't work."
> Others have looked to outer space as a potential source of life. Sir Fred Hoyle, convinced that life could not have originated on earth, suggested that it was brought here from space. While this panspermia view has its advocates, the naturalistic answer to how life began on Earth remains as elusive as ever.

FROM DUST TO DUST

It was the eminent scientist, Stephen Hawking, who said, "There have been various ideas, but for me the most attractive is that the universe was spontaneously created out of absolutely nothing."[8] So it's not too difficult for someone to take that a step further and believe that it was *God* who spontaneously created the universe from absolutely nothing.

But the Book of Genesis goes on to tell us that God then made man from the *soil* of the earth. What an embarrassingly unscientific statement...so it seems. According to Yale University, the elements that make up the soil are: 1. Potassium, 2. Calcium, 3. Magnesium, 4. Phosphorous, 5. Iron, and 6. Manganese.[9]

If God made the human body from the soil, it makes sense that both the soil and the body would be made up of the same elements. Let's then see if these six elements that are present in the soil are also in the human body:

1. Potassium plays an important role in...nerve transmission [and] in conversion of glucose into glycogen and muscle building.[10]

2. Calcium...is known as the fifth most common element in the earth's crust and is a primary mineral in the human body.[11]

3. Magnesium is essential to the functioning of the human body because it transmits nerve impulses, causes the contraction of muscles' and is integral to healthy development of teeth and bones.[12]

4. Phosphorus is present in bones and teeth and combines with calcium to form calcium phosphate which is the substance which gives the skeleton rigidity.[13]

5. Iron is a mineral found in every cell of the body.[14]

6. Manganese is an essential element to the human body...[15]

So, is it a coincidence that the same six elements that are in the soil are also essential for the life of the human body? That's what you and I have to figure out before death takes us into eternity...when our bodies decompose and turn back to the soil from which they came.

In answer to the question, "Did life begin in an "RNA world?" L.J. Gibson of the Geoscience Research Institute says:

> For many years there has been a general dissatisfaction with the protein hypothesis of the origin of life. Proteins cannot replicate themselves, making them unsuitable as a starting point for the development of life. However, there seemed to be no naturalistic alternative available until recently. This newer hypothesis has been dubbed the "RNA World" (Gilbert 1986). The basis for this model is the discovery that certain RNA molecules have catalytic properties. Since RNA also serves as a carrier of information, it seemed reasonable to suggest that ancient RNA molecules might have acted as a starting point for the origin of life. The "RNA World" hypothesis for the origin of life seems a significant improvement over the protein hypothesis, and has been the subject of considerable discussion.

His article concludes with:

> The "RNA World" hypothesis for the origin of life requires implausible events at each step in the sequence outlined. Small molecules are highly unlikely to have been available in any plausible model of a primordial earth. Even if small molecules were present, they would be highly unlikely to produce the large protein and nucleic-acid molecules useful for life. Even if the large molecules were present, there is

no known mechanism whereby they might be organized into functional cellular or subcellular units. The "RNA World" hypothesis suffers from many of the same problems as the protein hypothesis, and has additional problems of its own. Considering the conditions necessary for the establishment of life, it appears that the most plausible explanation for the origin of life is an intelligent creator."[16]

CHAPTER FOUR

INTELLECTUAL DEGRADATION

A S WE HAVE seen, man *cannot* create a grain of sand from nothing, let alone a living, breathing entity. He can manipulate, engineer, influence, or maneuver, but he cannot create a green pea, sheep, chickens, a pig, a tree, or even a flea, from nothing. Again, we know that with all of his genius, man cannot create anything from nothing, so how intellectually preposterous is it to actually believe that in the beginning nothing created everything? Atheism is off the charts of human folly. By contrast, the flat-earther is a real genius.

The moon has a lot of silica on its surface, which is a very reflective mineral, ideal for reflecting the sun. The moon turns at exactly the same speed it orbits, so we never see the other side. The sun and the moon govern the tides, the moon more than the sun since it is closer to earth. When the moon is close to earth the tides will be high in that region, since the gravitational pull of the moon pulls the water on earth towards it. The moon causes tides, which cause waves to break along shores (also waves at sea). This tumbling effect brings oxygen into the water, which keeps sea life alive. If the moon were larger or closer the tides would be devastating; if it were smaller or farther away the tides would fail to oxygenate the water and most sea life would die.

The moon governs our entire tidal system. Yet atheists, in the name of science, mock the thought that the moon can "rule the night" (see Genesis 1:16). Perhaps in time science will discover that the moon has a relationship to the night. Sadly, atheism has done to science what hypocrisy has done to Christianity.

When a man (or woman) professes atheism, he immediately disqualifies himself to speak as a representative of science because his premise is a violation of the fundamental rule of science.

Some evolutionists seem to think that I'm a monk and I live in some sort of monastery. But I'm not locked away from the real world. I go out for meals, follow the news, and read books. I also love science. In case you didn't know, "science" is God allowing man to discover the secret workings of His incredible creation. Many of our greatest scientists loved God—Galileo, Newton, Francis Bacon, Nicholas Copernicus, Michael Faraday, Louis Pasteur, and Kepler, just to name a few. Einstein (a theist who didn't believe in a *personal* God), rightly said, "Science without religion is lame; religion without science is blind."

Einstein said, "I want to know how God created this world... I want to know His thoughts, the rest are details." If you also want to know God's thoughts, read your Bible.

My Christian friends also love science. Without it they would be blind, as Einstein said. But look what he said about those who leave God out of the equation. They are lame. But they also intellectually disqualify themselves from speaking on behalf of science, because their basic worldview of "nothing created everything" is a scientific impossibility.

Einstein said, "I want to know how God created this world, I am not interested in this or that phenomenon, in the spectrum of this or that element. I want to know His thoughts, the rest are details."[1] If you also want to know God's thoughts, read your Bible.

An atheist speaks of the incredible creation. I speak of the incredible Creator. He speaks of the greatness of space. I speak of the greatness of the One who made it. He loves creation. I love the Creator and will escape His terrible swift sword, because I trust in His mercy. It's my earnest prayer that every human being would also trust Jesus for his own eternal salvation.

MY "DISHONESTY" AND EVOLUTION

Atheists and evolutionists are continually accusing me of dishonesty because I want evidence of species-to-species transition forms. They say that I don't understand the true evolutionary theory.

Let's settle this argument once and for all. The "missing link" is something that links one species changing into another species. The following article addresses the subject. In it, I have italicized references to species-to-species transitional forms:

Discovered: the missing link that solves a mystery of evolution. Scientists have made one of the most important fossil finds in history: a missing link *between fish and land animals* [change from one species to another species], showing how creatures first walked out of the water and on to dry land more than 375m years ago. Paleontologists have said that the find, a crocodile-like animal called the *Tiktaalik roseae* and described today in the journal *Nature*, could become an icon of evolution in action—like *Archaeopteryx*, the famous fossil that bridged the gap *between reptiles and birds* [change from one species to another species]. As such, it will be a blow to proponents of intelligent design, who claim that the many gaps in the fossil record show evidence of some higher power.[2]

Of course, as touched on earlier, the above claims can't be substantiated. *Archaeopteryx* (unlike *Archaeoraptor*) is not a hoax —it is a bird, not a "missing link" between birds and reptiles. The missing link is still missing, and we're still waiting for the first piece of genuine evidence for the theory of evolution.

CONFESSIONS OF A BACKSLIDDEN ATHEIST

Atheist, novelist, and biographer A. N. Wilson, a friend of best-selling atheists Richard Dawkins and Christopher Hitchens, made the stunning announcement in April of 2009. He had become a believer in Jesus Christ.

Explaining his original embrace of atheism, Wilson said:

> As a hesitant, doubting, religious man I'd never known how they felt. But, as a born-again atheist, I now knew ex-actly what satisfactions were on offer. For the first time in my thirty-eight years I was at one with my own generation. I had become like one of the Billy Grahamites, only in reverse. If I bumped into Richard Dawkins (an old colleague from Oxford days) or had dinner in Washington with Christopher Hitchens…I did not have to feel out on a limb. Hitchens was excited to greet a new convert to his non-creed and put me through a catechism before uncorking some stupendous claret. "So—absolutely no God?" "Nope," I was able to say with Moonie-zeal. "No future life, nothing out there?" "No," I obediently replied. At last! I could join in the creed shared by so many (most?) of my intelligent contemporaries in the Western world—that men and women are purely material beings (whatever that is supposed to mean), that "this is all

there is" (ditto), that God, Jesus, and religion are a load of baloney: and worse than that, the cause of much (no, come on, let yourself go), most (why stint yourself—go for it, man), all the trouble in the world, from Jerusalem to Belfast, from Washington to Islamabad.

But then Wilson began to think, and the catalyst that made him think was the same one that started my brain working when I was twenty-one years old. The reality of death is a massive elephant in the room under and around which this unthinking world walks. A foot coming down full force on friends and loved ones tends to remind us that death is a level playing field. I could see the elephant and knew that it was just a matter of time for the foot to fall. Wilson continued:

> Watching a whole cluster of friends, and my own mother, die over quite a short space of time convinced me that purely materialist "explanations" for our mysterious human existence simply won't do—on an intellectual level. The phenomenon of language alone should give us pause. A materialist Darwinian was having dinner with me a few years ago and we laughingly alluded to how, as years go by, one forgets names. Eager, as committed Darwinians often are, to testify on any occasion, my friend asserted: "It is because when we were simply anthropoid apes, there was no need to distinguish between one another by giving names." This creedal confession struck me as just as superstitious as believing in the historicity of Noah's Ark. More so, really.

Creation cannot be divorced from a Creator. Its existence is testimony to Him who brought it into existence. Yet the professing atheist "suppresses the truth in unrighteousness."[3] He denies the axiomatic. Interestingly, it was the "evolution" of language that spoke to Wilson about God:

Do materialists really think that language just "evolved," like finches' beaks, or have they simply never thought about the matter rationally? Where's the evidence? How could it come about that human beings all agreed that particular grunts carried particular connotations? How could it have come about that groups of anthropoid apes developed the amazing morphological complexity of a single sentence, let alone the whole grammatical mystery which has engaged Chomsky and others in our lifetime and linguists for time out of mind? No, the existence of language is one of the many phenomena—of which love and music are the two strongest —which suggest that human beings are very much more than collections of meat. They convince me that we are spiritual beings, and that the religion of the incarnation, asserting that God made humanity in His image, and continually restores humanity in His image, is simply true. As a working blueprint for life, as a template against which to measure experience, it fits.

When I think about atheist friends, including my father, they seem to me like people who have no ear for music, or who have never been in love. It is not that (as they believe) they have rumbled the tremendous fraud of religion— prophets do that in every generation. Rather, these unbelievers are simply missing out on something that is not difficult to grasp. Perhaps it is too obvious to understand; obvious, as lovers feel it was obvious that they should have come together, or obvious as the final resolution of a fugue.

THE SECRET PLAN

My wife and I watched an old black-and-white version of Charles Dickens's *A Tale of Two Cities*, and I was moved to a point of tears. The story is set during the French Revolution and is about a young lawyer named Sydney Carton who loses the woman he loves to another man. Through a series of circumstances the woman's husband is awaiting the *guillotine*, and the lawyer gets into the prison, takes his place, and is executed, leaving the husband to go free and be with the one he loves.

Sadly, the movie dropped the fact that the hero was converted to Christianity during the last few days of his life, repeating the words of Jesus, "I am the resurrection and the life." In fact, resurrection is the dominant theme of the final part of the novel, but not in the movie. The husband is rescued at the last moment and recalled to life; Carton chooses death and resurrection to a life better than that which he has ever known.

What brought me to tears was the secret plan the hero contrived—to give his life for another. Such nobility is rare among humanity. It is the ultimate gift that we can give to another. No greater love has a man than this—that he should lay down his life for his friends.

"The existence of language is one of the many phenomena —of which love and music are the two strongest—which suggest that human beings are very much more than collections of meat."

Sadly, many see the suffering death of Jesus as simply an example of how we should live. We should live and die as Jesus lived and died—sacrificially. Yet His sinless life reveals how far we fall short of what we should be and in His suffering He was taking the punishment that we deserve. This was something I never understood until I saw my sin in its true light. Calvary is God's offer of mercy to guilty criminals, and that offer is meaningless until we see our guilt.

CHAPTER FIVE

IGNORANT KNUCKLE-DRAGGERS

A N ATHEIST once wrote: "I never said we were unreasoning animals; I said we were animals. If you deny that we are then you need to go take a basic science course." This statement reveals why the believer in the theory of evolution often has the convictions of a religious zealot. It also reveals why those who don't believe as they do are seen as ignorant knuckle-draggers. If evolution is true, then man is simply an animal. That means he is free to embark on his sexual prowls, because it is nothing but a basic instinct to do so. It's his procreative nature to fornicate, and therefore not a sin. For the atheist, understandably from his point of view, this is a hill to die on.

As one evolutionist said:

> We are humans, yes, we are apes too. What you seem to ignore is that classifications need levels of categories. For instance, chimps are chimps, just like humans are humans, and we both are apes (higher order of classification). The

ape equation, we being animals too, is a natural conclusion, nothing to do with being "sinners."

Evolution swings open a door for the evolutionist to do whatever he pleases, as long as what he does is within the bounds of a civil law he is ever expanding to accommodate his lower desires.

If man is an animal, he can justify homosexuality and even bestiality, because "other" animals do it. To him, evolution is a license to act like an animal.

The dictionary says that an animal is "any such living thing other than a human being." The word *human* means "lowly" or "frail," while *being* means that we are aware of our existence. We are unique among God's creation in that we are not only morally responsible, but we are aware that we are going to die.

I have spoken to countless atheists, and when pressed about the beginning, they say that they don't know the initial cause... but they choose to believe that it definitely wasn't God.

There is a basic instinct within all sane human beings that wants to live. So, let me concede slightly and let you call that desire "an animal instinct." So let's then obey our basic instinct—turn from our sins, trust in Jesus Christ, and God will make us fit to survive on the Day of Judgment.

The Bible says that the atheist is blind (see 2 Corinthians 4:3-4). What does that mean? To answer that, let me address the above question. The statement "There is no God" is an *absolute* statement. For an absolute statement to be true, we need absolute knowledge. If I said, "There is no gold in China," I need *absolute* knowledge that there is no gold in China. I need to know what's in every riverbed, in every rock, etc., because if there is one ounce of gold in China, my statement is false. However, I simply need to have seen a Chinese person in China yawn and see his gold tooth to know that there is gold in China.

"There is no God" is an absolute statement and can be said only by someone who possesses omniscience (all knowledge). The best a professing atheist can say is, "With the limited knowledge I have at present, I believe that there is no God, but I really don't know." The Christian, however, can know that God exists because he doesn't need all knowledge. He simply has to come to know Him experientially (an experience commonly known as "conversion").

If the professing atheist could see that the Christian doesn't "believe" in God, the argument about His existence would be over. I used to "believe" in God before my conversion. I looked at creation and believed that "in the beginning" there was a Creator because *reason* told me that creation could not create itself. *If it didn't exist before it came into being, how could it create itself?* It had to have come about by an eternal force, commonly known as "God."

I have spoken to countless atheists, and when pressed about the beginning, they say that they don't know the initial cause. They don't know, but they choose to believe that it definitely wasn't God. That's their choice.

However, the key word in this argument is the word "faith." Dictionary.com gives nine meanings for the word. Here is one: "Christian Theology. The trust in God and in His promises as made through Christ and the Scriptures by which humans are justified or saved." This is a "trust," as opposed to an intellectual "belief."

There is an analogy that clearly pulls this together. I can intellectually "believe" that a parachute will save me, but if I don't put it on, my faith is dead. The parachute won't help me at all. However, if I trust it (put it on), then it becomes beneficial. It saves me from the consequences of a ten-thousand-foot fall.

In the same way, I can intellectually believe in God's existence, but that type of faith won't benefit me at all. To be saved I have to *trust* in the person of Jesus Christ as my Savior. I have to, as the Bible says, "put on the Lord Jesus Christ." When I come to know the Lord, the argument about His existence is over.

But watch what comes back from professing atheists. They can't see the absolute simplicity of the issue. The Bible is so right. Atheists are blind, and this blindness is willful. They cannot see because they don't want to see.

The Ethics of the Average Atheist

"What do I mean when I express the hope that my ethical code is better than that espoused by the religious? I mean that I hope my ethics have the practical results of causing less harm to life and liberty, and dealing justice as humanely as possible, than any ethical teachings of any church."

The Christian's eternal salvation (the fact that he has eternal life) has got nothing to do with his being "good" or having an ethical code. If a criminal is shown mercy by a good judge and his case is dismissed, it wasn't dismissed on the basis of the criminal's goodness or his standard of ethics. It was entirely on the basis of the goodness of the *judge*. The sinner (a criminal in God's eyes) has his case dismissed (has his sins forgiven) because of God's goodness, not because of anything he has done.

Then, if the criminal has truly seen the kindness of the judge, he will leave his unlawful life behind him. This is done entirely out of appreciation for the judge's goodness in dismissing his case. That is the gospel in a nutshell. I was guilty of violating God's Law—which says that He sees lust as adultery, hatred as murder. His ethical standards are so high, lying lips are an "abomination" (extremely detestable) to Him. Yet His amazing grace (mercy) dismissed the case of a wretch like me.

I now live an ethical life out of an appreciation for mercy. This ethical life may or may not be as ethical as that of an atheist, but that will have no bearing at all on Judgment Day. God will judge the world in perfect righteousness, and only those who have called upon His mercy will be saved from His terrible justice.

It was Sir Isaac Newton who said: "I have a fundamental belief in the Bible as the Word of God, written by men who were inspired. I study the Bible daily. Opposition to godliness is atheism in profession and idolatry in practice. Atheism is so senseless and odious to mankind that it never had many professors."

Still, there are atheists who do have legitimate difficulties. One wrote: "What does the Bible have to say about the countless people who, through zero fault of their own, never hear the word of God? Do they go to Heaven or Hell?"

Those who have never heard the good news of the Gospel will go to Heaven, *if they have never sinned.* However, if they have ever lied, stolen, committed adultery, been covetous, had sex outside of marriage, looked with lust, hated anyone, been unthankful to God, committed homosexual acts, murdered, blasphemed, failed to love their neighbor as themselves, or failed to love the One who gave them life with all of their heart, soul, mind, and strength, etc., then they will end up in Hell. God will give them justice.

The problem is they have sinned (all of us have), and so they *desperately* need God's mercy. So, as Christians, we have a tremendous moral obligation to make sure that they are warned of their danger before they die (see Ezekiel 33:8, Romans 10:14-15). We must plead with those that the Bible calls "unsaved" to come to their senses. We should be as the disciples who, when they were threatened for preaching the Gospel, said, "We cannot but speak the things we have seen and heard."

Fortunately, you are not one of those who have never heard. You know that Jesus suffered and died for you. He paid your fine in His life's blood so that you could leave the Courtroom. That means that God can legally dismiss your case. Now, because of the suffering death and the resurrection of Jesus Christ, God can allow you to live and escape the damnation of Hell. What you must do to receive that mercy is repent and trust Him. Once you do that, you can take the Gospel to those for whom you are so concerned.

Another asked:

> Had any of you been born in Saudi Arabia, Iraq, Iran, Jordan, Syria, etc, there is nearly a 100 percent chance that you would be Muslim, and no amount of free will given to you from Jesus would prevent that. You would be doomed to Hell strictly because your parents lived in the wrong country. Think about that the next time you picture your God as all-loving and merciful. If He exists like you say He does, He is allowing millions of souls to go to Hell because they were born into a nation that does not believe in Him. How do you justify this?

God is not all-loving and merciful. To say that that is the sole makeup of His character is to create an idol. That god doesn't exist except in the minds of those that conceive Him to be like that. The God of the Bible is holy, righteous, full of justice and truth, as well as love and mercy.

The Law of God is the key to understanding the dealings of God with humanity. The Moral Law (the Ten Commandments) shows us that God is morally perfect, and because of His love of justice, He must by nature punish wrongdoing. If a man murders, justice must be done. If a man rapes, steals, commits adultery, lies, covets, etc., God's justice hovers over him. Once the Law comes into the equation it shows us that He owes humanity nothing but justice. He has no obligation to bless us with health or save us from death. All that comes by His mercy, something that doesn't come because we deserve it but because God is merciful.

So, if God sees fit to save someone in America, He does so because of His goodness. If He saves someone in Iraq, India, China, or Japan, He does so because He is good, and He reveals His goodness by sending missionaries to those countries so that they will hear the Gospel. Some countries forbid Christian missionaries from proclaiming the message of everlasting life. Other countries permit it.

The Bible says that no one comes to the Son unless the Father draws Him, and God draws whom He will to Himself whether the person to whom He is extending mercy lives in Iraq, New Zealand, China, Japan, or the United States.

But don't use that fact as an excuse to stay in your sins. That's not an option.

Scripture tells us that He commands every one of us to repent (see Acts 17:30-31), because He has appointed a day in which He will judge the world in righteousness.

PROBLEMS WITH THE BIBLE

Recently an atheist gave me a sheet of paper that listed his problems with the Bible. Heading the list was 1 Corinthians 1:26, a verse which he said proved that atheists are smarter than Christians.

Here is the verse: "For you see your calling, brethren, how that not many wise men after the flesh, not many mighty, not many noble, are called."

He seemed to have skipped over the words "after the flesh." There are different types of wisdom. There is the wisdom of this world ("after the flesh"), and there is the wisdom of God. The message of the passage is that God has chosen a seemingly foolish message of childlike faith to confound those proud folks who think that they are wise.

So if you look around the Christian faith, you won't find many of those proud people who are puffed up in their own "fleshly" wisdom. So the wisest of atheists isn't wiser than the dumbest of Christians. Rather, according to the Bible, he or she is a fool (see Psalm 14:1).

Also on the list was a reference to Jephthah, saying that he sacrificed his daughter. Somehow my atheist friend (and he is a friend) thought that, just because the Bible related the incident, God was somehow condoning it. He looked a little taken back when I told him that Jephthah was lacking a little in intellectual capacity. What he did was stupid.

The Scriptures are given to us for our instruction. We can learn life lessons from all the stupid things that men and women did in the Bible.

The Scriptures are given to us for our instruction. We can learn life lessons from all the stupid things that men and women did in the Bible. Noah became drunk and shamed himself. Saul became jealous and destroyed his life. Judas was a hypocrite and ended up killing himself. Peter slept when he should have been in prayer and denied his Lord. David let lust into his heart and committed adultery then murder. These incidents were written for our admonition and we can either humbly learn from them or proudly walk down the same tragic path. The choice is ours.

Do you know what I am trying to communicate with you? It's that you have a deadly, terminal, terrible disease called "sin," and that will be the death of you. I know that you don't believe that. You truly think that you are healthy when you are not. Time will show you the truth of what I am saying, if you let it.

So you tell the good doctor not to mention the symptoms of the disease because they are not pleasant. You would rather he says "ear-tickling" words to his patient.

Any doctor worth his salt will tell you the truth. He will even stick a sharp and painful needle into your wound if he thinks that it will save you from a terrible death. What you see as disparagement is in truth a love and concern for your eternal salvation. You may not see that today, but one day you may. That's my hope.

My mission as a Christian is to tell you what you don't want to hear—the truth that you have sinned against God and that the Bible says, "We are all as an unclean thing, and our righteousnesses (the best we can offer God) are as filthy rags." This is good news, because it means that there is nothing we can do to save ourselves from death, but turn to Him who will save us, because of the cross.

I don't want you to adopt my worldview. I just want you to be saved from death and Hell. Nothing else.

CHAPTER SIX

THE DINOSAUR IN THE BIBLE

MANY TIMES skeptics have pointed to the fact that the dinosaur existed as proof that God doesn't. They think that the Scriptures are silent on the subject, but, in what is said to be the oldest book of the Bible, God Himself speaks and talks about an amazing and massive creature.

Look closely at this portion of Scripture from Job 40:15-24 and visualize the creature being described:

Verse 15: "Behold now behemoth...." Some commentators have in the past believed that the "behemoth" is a reference to a hippopotamus. With due respect, that is ridiculous. This creature moves his tail "like a cedar." A hippopotamus doesn't have a tail that is like a large tree (see verse 17). It's more like a small twig.

Verse 15: "[W]hich I made with you; he eats grass as an ox."

What Did Dinosaurs Eat? "Although some fans of carnivorous 'Tyrannosaurus rex' and 'Velociraptor' may find it a bit disappointing—the vast majority of dinosaurs were plant-eaters. Most plant-eating dinosaurs had peg-like or broad, flat teeth designed for snipping or stripping vegetation."[1]

Verse 16: "Lo now, his strength is in his loins, and his force is in the navel of his belly." Study the structure of the dinosaur and you will see that its strength is in its huge leg and hip muscles (its loins).

Verse 17: "He moves his tail like a cedar…." A cedar is a massive tree. Skeptics, in an effort to discredit Scripture, have maintained that this is not a reference to an actual tail. However, the Hebrew word translated "tail" is *zanab* (Strong's 02180). In the Septuagint (the Greek translation of the Old Testament) the Greek word used here is *ouran*. This is the Greek word for "tail."

Verse 17: "[T]he sinews of his stones are wrapped together." "The word 'armor' is used to describe the hard, bony shell that some dinosaurs were covered with, rather like a crocodile's scaly skin or a tortoise's shell. Some of the best-protected dinosaurs were the plant-eating (herbivorous) ankylosauruses. A paleontologist called Torsten Scheyer from the University of Bonn has been looking at ankylosaurus fossils under a very strong microscope. He's been able to work out exactly how the armor was made and how strong it would have been. Torsten found that one type of ankylosaurus armor was made in exactly the same way as the materials for bullet-proof vests are made nowadays."[2]

Verse 18: "His bones are as strong pieces of brass; his bones are like bars of iron." "Interesting facts about dinosaur bones include its complexity as a skeletal network. Since dinosaurs are large creatures, their bones must be strong in order to support its massive weight and size" (www.dinosaur-facts.net). "Just one of Argentinosaurus's vertebrae was over four feet thick!" (http://dinosaurs.about.com).

Verse 19: "He is the chief of the ways of God…." This is the largest creature that God made: "The biggest dinosaur is probably ultrasauros. We only have a few bones of this late Jurassic [dated by evolutionists at 140 million years ago] plant-eater from

Colorado but they show an animal that was six stories high and may have weighed more than 50 tons" (www2.scholastic.com).

Verse 19: "He that made him can make his sword to approach unto him." "Although this mass extinction didn't happen literally overnight, in evolutionary terms, it may as well have—within a few thousand years of whatever catastrophe caused their demise, the dinosaurs had been wiped off the face of the earth."[3]

It is no mystery as to why the dinosaur disappeared. The dinosaur's Creator made his sword to approach him. Verse 20-23: "Surely the mountains bring him forth food, where all the beasts of the field play. He lies under the shady trees, in the covert of the reed, and fens. The shady trees cover him with their shadow; the willows of the brook compass him about. Behold, he drinks up a river, and hastens not: he trusts that he can draw up Jordan into his mouth."

Verse 24: "He takes it with his eyes: his nose pierces through snares." This, the biggest creature God ever made, was so tall its nose broke through tree branches: "Although paleontologists claim to have found bigger dinosaurs, Argentinosaurus is the biggest sauropod (four-footed herbivorous dinosaur) whose size is backed up by convincing evidence. This plant-muncher (named after Argentina, where its remains were found) measured about 120 feet from head to tail and weighed over 100 tons."[4]

What more evidence could any skeptic want that the Bible is inspired by God? Don't believe all the absurdity that skeptics say about bats not being birds, other untruths such as the Bible saying that the world is flat, and the mockery of Israel's judicial system. Every one of these many weak arguments has rational explanations for those who are prepared to soften their hearts and listen. There is too much at stake for the skeptic to embrace small-minded arguments as though they were the gospel truth.

The Bible proves itself to be the Word of God, not just because of its scientific, prophetic, and historically accurate facts, but because it points to Him who is knowable and grants everlasting life to all who trust in the Savior. It is the fact that God manifests Himself (see John 14:21) to all who call upon His name that is the ultimate proof of the truth of His Word.

THE WHALE

After reading what I had said about the Scriptures speaking of the dinosaur, someone said:

> We started out okay. Sort of. Ray even provided citations. Sort of. That could be a first. But then we got to Verse 19: "He is the chief of the ways of God…" This confirms that the dinosaur (or some dinosaur, anyway) was the largest creature that God made??? Really, that's what that verse means??? By the way, the Blue Whale is the largest. Goodness sakes, I knew that when I was in 4th grade.

Unfortunately, the fourth grade teacher was wrong:

> The Whale: "Blues whales are so big they are the biggest creature ever to have lived on earth—even bigger than the biggest dinosaurs! [They are wrong about this. See the below quote about how dinosaurs are bigger]. The largest whale ever measured was a female weighing 171,000 kgs and measuring over 90 ft. The longest whale measured in at over 110ft."[5]

> The Dinosaur: "This plant-muncher (named after Argentina, where its remains were found) measured about 120 feet from head to tail and weighed over 100 tons."[6]

Don't believe everything your teacher tells you. Especially when it comes to the unscientific theory of evolution. Keep in mind that Albert Einstein said: "In the view of such harmony in the cosmos which I, with my limited human mind, am able to recognize, there are yet people who say there is no God. But what makes me really angry is that they quote me for support of such views."[7]

I care what Einstein liked (and believed) because his name epitomizes intelligence. It is synonymous with the word "genius." Atheists say that intelligent design isn't intelligent and that anyone who believes that God exists hates science. So, although Albert Einstein's view of God is different than mine (he didn't believe in a *personal* God), it is pleasing to me that he humbly acknowledged the One who gave him life. He was no fool.

I have a little in common with Einstein. We are both Jewish. We both immigrated to the United States. We both believe that we were intelligently designed by God.

I have a little in common with Einstein. We are both Jewish. We both immigrated to the United States. We both believe that we were intelligently designed by God. We are both regularly misquoted by atheists. We both have moustaches. We both kept our hair, and mine has been known to look like his after a restless night's sleep.

Many times I have been told that I look like Albert Einstein. A few years ago when I was in Phoenix airport boarding a flight to Los Angeles, I gave million-dollar-bill tracts to four Muslim women and a little girl who was traveling with them. They were grateful, and told me that I looked like Einstein.

As they passed me on the plane, I heard them say, "There's Einstein." I have to say, it puffed me up a little, to think that they perceived an intellectual likeness. When we landed in Los Angeles, the little girl walked passed my seat and said in a friendly (and loud) voice "Goodbye, Frankenstein."

A friend even wrote a song about me, in which there was the line: "When you see a man riding a boy's bike; when you see an Einstein look-alike…"

There's only one thing in which I believe I trump the man. In 1982 I found something in the Scriptures that is infinitely more important and has far greater repercussions than the Theory of Relativity. So I think I have more in common with the great genius than most. One other thing: Intellectually, I'm not worthy to wash his socks. But I guess you already figured that. He also said:

> I'm not an atheist and I don't think I can call myself a pantheist. We are in the position of a little child entering a huge library filled with books in many different languages. The child knows someone must have written those books. It does not know how. The child dimly suspects a mysterious order in the arrangement of the books but doesn't know what it is. That, it seems to me, is the attitude of even the most intelligent human being toward God."[8]

CHAPTER SEVEN

THE BLIND FAITH OF THE THEORY OF EVOLUTION

I T IS COMMONLY accepted that the natural phenomenon of evolution had no end in mind when it created all living things. So it was fortunate for us that gravity just happened to be around to stop everything from spinning into space. But if evolution had nothing to do with gravity, who or what created it? "Chance" or "accident" is too big a leap of blind faith for me. The evolutionist's version of "just believe" isn't good enough. I want verifiable, scientific facts.

And while we are looking for facts, I would like evolutionists to explain to me where the other laws that govern the universe came from: i.e., the laws of thermodynamics, of motion, of heat. Why don't we see chaos everywhere instead of order?

Of course the "scientific" answer will be "We don't yet know where they came from, but one thing we are sure of, God didn't create them."

It was Newton's law of gravitation that showed science that the gravitational constant is in direct proportion to the product of the masses divided by the square of the distance apart. However, that doesn't explain the nature of gravity. Despite its mystery, the brilliant Newton attributed gravity's origin to the genius of Almighty God. So do I.

When Ben Stein[1] was asked why he hosted the movie *Expelled*, he said:

> Well, if there's no intelligent design, where did gravity come from? Where did thermodynamics come from? Where did the laws of motion and mechanics and fluid motion come from?...I could easily see evolution in species, but where did the great laws of the universe and of movement, the governing universe come from? And I thought, well, that's a really good question and yet, if you even ask that question, you can be disciplined in the academic setting.[2]

I appreciated his "you can be disciplined in the academic setting" for asking. I have been mocked by evolutionists for asking "where" gravity came from. Their answer is that it didn't come from anywhere. It just is.

LIKE THE BACK OF MY HAND

Have you ever taken the time to study closely the human hand? Let's set aside the issue of whether or not it happened by a process of evolution or was the result of intelligent design and just look at it for what it is.

The hand is a marvel of incredible technology. It is fearfully and wonderfully made. It can be used for brute force, like the wielding of a hammer, or for the intricate threading of a tiny needle.

We only have two hands while primates are often said to have four. This is because the primate's toes are long and the big toe is opposable and looks more like a thumb, thus enabling the feet to be used as hands. Try swinging from a tree branch using the soles of your feet, and you will see what I mean.

Look at the back of your left hand for a moment, if you have one handy. Study the fingernails and think about where they grow from, the shape in which each one grows, their substance, and how strange your hand would look without them.

Then look at your thumb. The stubby little fellow can be easily rotated 90 degrees on a level perpendicular to the palm, unlike the other fingers which can be rotated only approximately 45 degrees.

Look at the knuckles, and how the skin has folds on it at the right places to accommodate the bend of the fingers and thumb.

Each hand has twenty-seven bones, a massive freeway of various veins, life-giving warm blood, intricate overlapping muscles and tough tendons, and it's all

I have been mocked by evolutionists for asking "where" gravity came from. Their answer is that it didn't come from anywhere. It just is.

held together with flexible strong, yet soft, skin. The hand is connected to the arm, and the arm is connected to the shoulder, right up to central control—the brain, which tells the hand what to do and when to do it. And your marvelous hand is just a small part of the intricate human body, and the human body is just a small part of this amazing earth, and this incredible earth is but a tiny speck in this infinite universe.

If evolution is responsible for our hands and the rest of creation, we should fall at its wondrous feet in absolute homage. We should praise and adore it, and live in admiration of its power and ability. We are morally obliged to fall down in worship for its goodness in giving us the awe-inspiring gift of life. It is only right that we love evolution with all of our heart, mind, soul, and strength. Many do. It's called "idolatry."

DIRTY ROBERT

Late in 2008, I saw a homeless man lying on the sidewalk. I didn't stop to give him any money because I thought he might be insane. He sure looked it. Besides, he would probably use it for buying alcohol or cigarettes. But I began to think about my thoughts. Were they just excuses? How horrible if the man was insane. Imagine being tormented by a sick mind. I concluded that he may have needed money more than a sane person.

I went back and as I approached him his eyes flashed at me. His skin was ingrained with grime. He smelled like a filthy public restroom. I said, "Excuse me, sir. Are you okay? I would like to give you $20." He reached out his grimy hand, took the money, and without saying a word, he waved his hand in a gesture of appreciation. As I walked away I thought that my $20 was pretty pathetic. So I returned and gave him some more. As I walked away a second time, two men who had been watching me from across the street called out "Take him to a park!" They didn't want him living opposite their house. Sadly, I could understand their point of view.

I got up very early the next morning and rode my bike back toward the same spot. I had an agenda. I would offer to give the man a nice hot shower. While he was showering, I would go to a store and buy him some nice clean clothes. Then, we would go to the local barbershop and give him a haircut and shave. Then I would prepay for a room in a hotel for a week. From there we would go to a place I knew of that sold chickens, rabbits, and grain and ask if they would give him a job if I gave them his first week's wages. I was excited when I turned the corner and saw that he was still on the sidewalk.

I approached him, squatted beside him, and reminded him of our encounter the night before. He remembered me and said that his name was Robert and that he was sixty years old. I was pleased to find that he was coherent, but his speech was strangely quiet and deliberate.

I asked if he would like to get cleaned up, get a job, and have a roof over his head. I would pay for everything. Think of it—clean clothes, a job, and a warm room in a hotel. Robert went very quiet for a long time. I repeated my offer. He mumbled, "I'm thinking…" A moment later, he shook his head.

It turned out that he didn't mind his filth. He got a pension from the government and he got his clothes from a Goodwill store (many years ago, by the look and smell of them). I then shared the Gospel with him and left him on the sidewalk.

I was so disappointed. How sad that a human being chose to live like that, sitting in his own filth. He was so used it. I guess it seemed to be right and normal for him to do so.

The unbeliever is the same as Robert. He is like the Prodigal Son (see Luke 15:11-32) as he sits in the filth of his sins thinking that his unclean desires are normal and right. Yet through the Gospel God offers to wash him clean of his sins, give him a purpose in existence, and put an eternal roof over his head. Yet he chooses death over life, darkness over light, Hell over Heaven, all because he loves his sin and hates righteousness. What an unspeakable tragedy.

SECULAR PHILOSOPHY

A professing atheist can't be sure of anything. He doesn't know that there is no God. He doesn't know if Hell is a reality. If you are an atheist, all you have is your beliefs (faith) that God and Hell don't exist. You have faith in what you believe. You can't be sure that the sky is blue (it's not—it has no color) or that the sun rises (it doesn't—the earth turns). You don't know for certain that the blue or the red that you see is actually the same color that others see. You don't know if evolution is true or even if a rock is "hard," because you have no concrete definition of what "hard" is other than what a dictionary tells you and what you have come to believe from the beliefs of others. For all you know, you might be insane and have twisted perceptions of what others see as reality. That's why knowing God is such a wonderful thing. It's because He knows the thoughts of everyone that has ever existed, and He is ever-present on every planet to determine if there are or are not green leprechauns.

The Scriptures give us insight into the mind of God. Through them we can know absolute truth. We can know reality. We have what the Bible calls "an anchor for the soul." He is the rock of sanity. Without the solid foundation of the Word of God you will be blown about by the winds of an ever-changing secular philosophy.

The truth is that the Christian is like a doctor working with a patient who has psychological problems. The doctor has been well trained to recognize that his patient suffers from delusional paranoia (thinking that the good doctor wants to harm him).

You may think that I am too strong with my words, but it's not me that calls the professing atheist a "fool." It is God's Word —"The fool has said in his heart, 'There is no God'" (Psalm 14:1). It's not me that says that he is prideful; it's the Word of God. It says that it is the pride of his face that is stopping him from seeking God. It even reveals that it's not that he cannot find Him, but that he *will* not (see Psalm 10:4). In other words it's a matter of our will—we don't want God.

Who would have believed that any human being would ever have to try and prove to any other human being that we were created? It is evidence that we live in a world of insanity where it has become commonplace for fathers to murder their children, husbands to beat their wives, kids to kill kids at school. It is an insane world where people breathe in carcinogens in the form of a cigarette and feel cool, where it's normal and good to poison yourself through alcoholic intoxication, where lying and stealing are acceptable behavior.

We live in a world where mothers kill their children before they are born, where priests in the name of God molest children, and where so-called rational people believe that we are related to primates and call such unfounded imaginations "science."

And yet there is an insanity that rises above all this craziness. It is the ultimate psychosis. God offers everlasting life to all who trust and obey Him, and the insane mock Him and His Word. The Bible says that when we come to Christ we receive a "sound" mind. Until then, the insane live on undiagnosed. I am speaking of myself also. I lived to twenty-two years without thinking at all about the issues of life and death, God and eternity.

The Bible reveals the root cause of all this mess. The issue has nothing to do with science. It is a corruption that the Bible calls "sin." The essence of sin is a rebellion against our Creator. It's an evil that dwells within each of us, refusing to yield to His moral government. We are like rebels who have hijacked a plane that we have no idea how to fly. We are plummeting toward the ground with no hope of salvation, and yet the Control Tower offers to guide us to safety. That's the core of conversion—a total yielding of the controls back to the lawful Owner.

We justly deserve death. God offers us everlasting life. Please repent today. Apologize to God for your transgressions of His Law. Think about your sins then think about the Savior. Think about what He did for you on the cross. Trust Jesus Christ—give Him total control, and you will have the ultimate promise from God Who "cannot lie." He will save you from death.

Sheep in Wolf's Clothing

Do Christians make you nervous? Are you afraid of our political aspirations? Do you want to keep us out of the education system? Do you think we are narrow-minded and dangerous? I know that many of you do.

Being born of the Spirit (see John 3) lifts us up out of the confines of the natural world and allows us to think outside of the box.

You think that we have an evil agenda, and you are concerned because we are everywhere, and that gives us political power. We are doctors, nurses, mechanics, scientists, pilots, and authors, and some of us are even politicians.

Genuine Christians really are quite harmless. We are likened to sheep (see John 10), and sheep don't normally attack people. I did a quick search on the Internet, using the search words "Sheep attacks man," and came up with only two clips. One was a sheep following a boy rather than attacking him, and the other was funny more than anything. Dogs are called "man's best friend," yet they attack and sometimes kill people. It is estimated that 2 percent of the U.S. population, an amazing 4.7 million people, are bitten by dogs each year. Chimpanzees, elephants, bears, lions, tigers, and other animals attack and kill people. But sheep don't.

You may think that we are wolves in sheep's clothing, but we're not. We are not out to kill you, or bite you, or hurt you in the slightest. We love you, and our deepest desire is for you to find the gift of everlasting life, and you will find that only by following the Good Shepherd.

LIFT THE LID

A friend gave us nine chickens recently. They were just five days old when we got them, and since it's been a long time since our three kids left the roost, it's been great fun for Sue and me to watch these little birds grow and spread their wings. We will keep them inside under a heat lamp until they're mature enough to go into our chicken coop along with their aunts. No doubt we will see some infighting when that happens as they go through their pecking order.

I remember watching one chick that ventured outside of the small world in which she lived. She jumped up onto the side of the tall box and she sat and gazed at what must have looked like a massive living room.

I couldn't help thinking how tiny her world has been since she was born (hatched). Her whole existence was nothing more than a box, a heat lamp, eight of her buddies, food, and water to drink.

It made me think of some people I know who are confined to the small box of the atheist worldview. Their philosophy of "I have no belief in a God" shuts out the eternal and the infinite. It confines them to the natural world, when there is a massive living room of the Supernatural surrounding them. Being born of the Spirit (see John 3) lifts us up out of the confines of the natural world and allows us to think outside of the box.

All it takes to get out is a leap of faith. Talk of faith may make you nervous, but you won't be disappointed if you repent first, then couple that repentance with simple trust in the Savior. Please do it. Unless you are chicken.

A group of onlookers once stared at a luxury liner and could not believe what they saw. Some passengers had dived into the sea and were clinging to a lifeboat while the rest of the passengers who stayed on board were laughing at them.

The onlookers remarked to each other how foolish they were to dive off the boat. Then the great liner hit something under the sea, sunk in moments and dragged all those who stayed on board down with it.

Suddenly they realized that those who looked like fools were wise, and those who stayed on the ship and looked liked they were wise, were actually fools.

We know that we look like bird-brained fools because we have left the pleasures of this sinful world and cling to Jesus Christ. But we also know that the time will come when we will be seen to be wise, and those who seem to be wise will be shown to be fools. It's far better to be a bird-brain than a dead dog.

THE ELDERLY LADY

But how could God send a sweet elderly lady to Hell? Say you knew a ninety-five-year-old lady who was a wonderful person, who never said an unkind word to a soul. Then I have to ask how you knew that in her ninety-five years she never said a harsh word to a soul. Perhaps you are being charitable yourself and kindly giving your friend the benefit of the doubt. But let's say that she was almost morally perfect, except for three slips a day. Just three times each twenty-four hours did she perhaps think a lustful thought, or fail to love God with her heart, mind, soul, and strength, or fail to love her neighbor (everyone) as much as she loved herself (which is the essence of the requirement of God's Law). Maybe she became angry without cause, or was greedy, unthankful to God, or selfish. But she slipped only three times each day. So she sins against God a thousand times a year. If we take a count from the age of ten, that's eighty-five thousand sins (crimes against His Law) that God has seen and must punish because of His perfect holiness.

Most of us would sin ten times as much as that with our lustful, selfish, self-righteous, unthankful, and greedy thoughts, as well as our lying, stealing, blasphemy, and failing to do what we know we should. That's why the Bible says that each of us has a "multitude" of sins (see James 5:20).

So if your elderly friend was as perfect as you say she was, she doesn't need a Savior. She will be fine on Judgment Day. However, if she was like the rest of us, and she actually became pious in her old age because she was driven by a guilty conscience, she desperately needed God's forgiveness. And she could have found that in the person of Jesus Christ.

God promised that He would liberate the human race from death and that He would do this through the suffering death of the Jewish Messiah (see Isaiah 53). The result would be peace with God for all who would humble themselves, repent, and trust the God-given Savior (see Isaiah 55:1-3). Peace with God would mean everlasting life for humanity.

The Old Testament said that the result of conversion would be a new heart with new desires—desires to please the God with Whom we were once at enmity (a "heart of stone" towards Him): "I will give you a new heart and put a new spirit within you; I will take the heart of stone out of your flesh and give you a heart of flesh. I will put My Spirit within you and cause you to walk in My statutes, and you will keep My judgments and do them" (Ezekiel 36:25-27).

The salvation of God (eternal life) would be offered to all men: to the Jew first, then to the Greek, the Indian, as well as the Chinese, Russian, Muslim, Hindu, Buddhist, Kiwi, Aussie, and even atheist—those who are red and yellow, black and white, all are precious in His sight. Anyone can be saved from death and Hell (see Romans 10:13). There is only one stipulation. They must come through the God-provided Savior, not through a man-made religion which cannot wash away sin. Jesus Christ is the only One who can forgive sin and give peace with God because He was God manifest in human form.

There is a big reason for this exclusivity. All man-made religions are "works righteous" religions. Their adherents think that they can get to Heaven by being good, praying, fasting, doing good works, repenting, etc. (see Romans 10:2-3). This is because they don't understand one very important truth: God is utterly perfect. His Law therefore demands moral perfection. It says that lust is adultery in His eyes and hatred is murder. His Moral Law (the Ten Commandments) shows us that He is a Judge and that we are all desperate criminals in His sight. That changes everything. Now, anything we offer the Judge isn't "good works," but a despicable attempt to bribe Him, and that is an abomination in His sight (see Proverbs 21:27). The only thing that can save us is the mercy of the Judge.

> *All man-made religions are "works righteous" religions. Their adherents think that they can get to Heaven by praying, fasting, doing good works, repenting, etc.*

Fortunately, we are told that God is "rich" in mercy. In His kindness He provided a Savior—someone to pay our fine in His life's blood. That happened at the Cross.

This is what that Savior said about Himself: "I am the way, the truth and the life. No man comes to the Father but through Me" (John 14:6). Old and New Testament Scripture is consistent:

"They shall be My people, and I will be their God; then I will give them one heart and one way, that they may fear Me forever, for the good of them and their children after them" (Jeremiah 32:38), "Nor is there salvation in any other, for there is no other name under heaven given among men by which we must be saved" (Acts 4:12).

Tragically, whoever dies in their sins will get fearful justice. Whoever dies in Christ will have mercy and thus have everlasting life. It's very simple. See Romans 2:6-9.

So let's not complain about God being unfair because people perish if they die in their sins. Instead, we should become missionaries and spend our lives telling this God-hating world the good news of eternal salvation for all humanity. I did.

CHAPTER EIGHT

THE STRAW MAN

A "STRAW MAN" argument is an informal fallacy based on misrepresentation of an opponent's position. Here is an example of an argument containing four straw man fallacies:

> If you were God and (1) your children here on earth (2) failed to trust in Jesus, (3) would you torture them eternally or just forgive them? Wouldn't you say "You broke the law but, you know what? It's impossible to keep. (4) I love you and I understand your lack of faith"?

All four points of this straw man argument misrepresent Christianity. When an evolutionist accuses someone of a straw man argument, however, the evolutionist has a problem. The theory of evolution is forever redefining itself, so he has no authoritative textbook to which he may refer. The Christian, however, has the unchanging Scriptures, making it very easy to blow over straw men created by skeptics.

First let's look at the misrepresentation of the relationship of man to God by the use of the phrase "your child here on earth." The people of the secular world are not God's children. The Bible says we are the devil's children. Satan is the god of this world and it is his will we do (see 2 Corinthians 4:4). We are enemies of God, rebels, who hate Him without cause. We are unthankful for His kindness and our hearts are deceitfully wicked (see Jeremiah 17:9). The Bible says we drink evil like water, and we are not God's children until we repent and trust the Savior. The moment we do that, we are born into His family and have the privilege of calling Him "Father."

The second fallacy is the phrase "failed to trust in Jesus." If a man jumps out of a plane and falls ten thousand feet to his death because he neglects to put on a parachute, he dies primarily because the force of gravity exerted weight upon the mass of his body. Had he put on a parachute he could have been saved from its unforgiving consequences, but again, he dies because by his own choice he caused the force of gravity to exert weight upon his body and spread him on the ground. The straw man argument is that it is unfair of God to punish someone for not doing something. However, "sin" according to the Bible is not a failure to trust Jesus, but "transgression of God's Law"—the Ten Commandments (see 1 John 3:4). Those who have the sense to "put on the Lord Jesus Christ" will be saved from violation of God's Law.

The third wording is also based on a lack of understanding. The straw man argument goes, "Would you torture them eternally or just forgive them?" When God's Law is left out of the equation, justice makes no sense. However, the Moral Law is eternal, absolute, and perfect. Think for a moment how tenacious we are when civil law is violated. A man rapes and kills three women, is tried, and is given the death sentence. He escapes. What does the law do? It spends millions of dollars to bring him to justice. Why? It doesn't bring the women back. Why doesn't the law simply forgive him? Because justice must be done.

Every human being has violated God's Law a multitude of times. We are unthankful and self-righteous. We lie, steal, and burn with lust. We are naturally selfish, hateful, and blasphemous fornicators. The Bible says that our eyes are "full of adultery," and that we are "filthy dreamers." We are more than worthy of the death sentence and damnation. So why doesn't God simply forgive us? Because justice must be done. If sinful man goes to great lengths to see that justice is done, how much more will a perfect and holy God make sure that every murderer, rapist, thief, and liar gets what is due to him? Hell is God's prison and those that go there will go there for life. There is no way out...not a hope in Hell.

Yet God (in His great mercy) has made a way for us to be freely forgiven for our wickedness. He became a Man in the person of Jesus of Nazareth and suffered and died on the cross. God's wrath came down on Him so that it wouldn't have to come down on us. He defeated death through the Resurrection and opened the door of everlasting life to all who would repent and trust in Him.

Is God's Law "impossible" to keep? It is for guilty sinners. How can we "keep" a Law we have already violated? However, we "keep" the Law when we trust in Jesus. Its demands were satisfied in Christ. It is appeased because our fine was paid by the Savior. That means that God can legally dismiss our case and commute our death sentence. We are at peace with the Law.

The fourth and final straw man that broke the camel's back also comes from a lack of understanding: It is "I love you and I understand your lack of faith." A judge may love a criminal but he cannot allow his love to interfere with justice. He must do that which is right despite his feelings for a criminal. Our straw man maker wants to cling to his belief that sin is simply a lack of faith and that he shouldn't be punished for not being able to believe something. However there are times in Scripture when Jesus rebuked His disciples for a lack of faith in Him and in the Scriptures. He called them "fools" and "slow of heart" to believe all that the prophets have spoken (see Luke 24:25). Such words are appropriate. Any man who doubts the instructions that tell him how to be saved from a ten-thousand-foot jump, and then fails to put on a parachute because of his doubts, is definitely a fool.

TESTABLE EVIDENCE

There are those who say, "God is not based upon observable, testable evidence. He is based upon faith. With God we are unable to make predictions and test them to see whether they are correct."

That is not true. Creation is "observable" evidence of the existence of God to all but a fool (again, the Bible says an atheist is a fool—See Psalm 14:1). God is not "based upon faith." Such a thought is ridiculous. His existence or nonexistence has nothing to do with whether or not I have faith. As with human relationships, the means of exchange between God and mankind is based on trust.

Anyone can make the prediction that God will manifest Himself to them and then they can test the prediction to see if it is valid. But there are two stipulations when coming to God. First they must believe that He exists. That makes sense. Why would anyone come to God if they didn't believe He existed? Again, in the light of creation, such a person would be a fool. And the second stipulation is that they have a humble heart. God resists the proud and gives grace to the humble. If they are proud, they have already cut themselves off from God by their sins. However, all those who humble themselves, repent, and trust in Jesus Christ come to know Him who is "life eternal." It's that simple.

UGLY AND HATEFUL RELIGION

A common argument from modern atheists is, "Any God that would torture Anne Frank for all eternity is unworthy of worship…" Awhile back, Ray posted a comment addressing the question of what happens to a child deep in the third world who dies w/o ever even hearing about Jesus? Does he get a break? Nope. Not according to your religion. I don't buy into hateful, ugly religions like that.

Jesus was Jewish. All the disciples were Jewish. The first eight thousand Christians were Jewish. I am Jewish. Christianity came from the home of the Jews. It went to "the Jew first," and is now universal to both Jew and Gentile. It isn't an American religion. It's Jewish. And, because God is so gracious, His Word says that "whoever" repents and trusts alone in Jesus Christ for his salvation is Heaven-bound. He has eternal life! It is that simple.

God is not "based upon faith." Such a thought is ridiculous. His existence or nonexistence has nothing to do with whether or not I have faith.

I would like to know how atheists know what Ann Frank believed about the promised Jewish Messiah. I would like them to explain to me how they can make such a harsh judgment about her salvation and think that she went to Hell.

And how do they know so much about this "third world" of which they speak (I presume that they think that they are part of the first world)? Their understanding of biblical theology is sadly very lacking. If they had it correct, they would know that God saves whom He will, whether they are in your third, second, or first world. He graciously saved me—a Jew, who lived at the uttermost part of the earth (fourth world country?).

The reason they don't buy into a "hateful, ugly religion" is that they have created their own ugly, hateful view of Christianity. It is blinding them to the reality of the love and forgiveness of God. It is as blinding as racial prejudice and *much* more damning.

WHY I DON'T EMBRACE THE FAITH OF RICHARD DAWKINS

Evolution has as much credibility with me as does the flying spaghetti monster. I am amazed at how many people can write so much about a subject that they insist is scientific, but that has no credible scientific basis. I speak as one that once embraced the thoughtless theory. What is also amazing is that its believers hide behind this pseudo-science and look condescendingly down on anyone who doesn't have the faith that they do. If you don't believe evolution, you are considered to be an intellectual knuckle-dragger.

The fact that so many supposedly learned men believe the theory reminds me that once upon a time most learned men believed in a flat earth. But their faith didn't change reality.

When it comes to evolution, I have asked for facts from those who believe its claims, and all I get is that you have to have faith in what has been taught. A good evolutionist believes without a doubt what his professor has told him. He *has* to believe when the pope of evolution, Professor Richard Dawkins, tells him: "You cannot be both sane and well educated and disbelieve in evolution. The evidence is so strong that any sane, educated person has got to believe in evolution."[1]

So unbelievers are insane and uneducated. But according to the learned professor, someone who doesn't believe is even worse than that. He also said: "It is absolutely safe to say that, if you meet somebody who claims not to believe in evolution, that person is ignorant, stupid or insane (or wicked, but I'd rather not consider that)."[2] So infidels (unbelievers) are actually wicked (sinful) if they don't believe in the theory of evolution. There's an example of sweeping judgmental intolerant fanaticism.

I have challenged Professor Dawkins to give me his best sermon on why I should believe in the theory he believes, and why he thinks that God "probably" doesn't exist. But he has a vow of silence when it comes to me, despite the fact that I said I would drop $20,000 in his personal collection plate.

Every day 150,000 people die. That's a fact of life. But each of us somehow thinks that death is something that happens to other people or at least it will come to us when we are in our late nineties. However, most men die in their early seventies. If you are fifty years old, you have around one thousand weekends left to live. If you are sixty, you have a mere five hundred. Professor Dawkins is sixty-eight years old! That's why I'm seriously pushing for a debate, because it's just a matter of time before he goes to meet his Maker.

Still, the devout follower of Dawkins and Darwin will believe anything said to him on believers' Web sites, or in believers' books. Evolution's many adherents simply fortify the truth that human beings are incredibly gullible and will believe anything as long as it's not in the Bible. How true are the words of Professor Dawkins when he said, "Faith is belief in spite of, even perhaps because of, the lack of evidence." He has unquestioning faith in evolution. I do not.

I hope that helps you to understand why I don't even give evolution a "pretense" of acknowledgement. To do so would be to be both disingenuous and foolish to the highest degree.

EVERY SINGLE ATOM

An atheist wrote, "I'm proud of my family and friends, also of my own achievements. Why is that wrong? Because it relegates God down the importance rung a little? We know He is a jealous God, He says so himself. God has had nothing to do with my achievements. I have never asked Him for help, nor according to Christian doctrine do I deserve help. So He gets no thanks. Not that I'd thank Him anyway—He's not real."

This sort of talk is similar to that of a teenager, who after receiving everything he has from his loving mother, stabs her in the back and says, "I have done nothing wrong." How could anyone reason for a moment with such a person? God gave us eyes to see with, ears to hear with, and a brain with which to think. Yet we are willfully blind, deaf, and dumb to that fact. Every atom that makes up our bodies and every drop of blood in our veins came from God. Everything that gives us the ability to achieve anything came only from the goodness of God.

Of course, the true atheist doesn't believe that. Neither does he believe in any initial cause. He believes that there's no God, no Maker, and no Creator. We didn't make ourselves, so he is stuck with the belief that nothing made everything "in the beginning" and time brought us to where we are now. It all happened because evolution did it. Sure.

How applicable is Scripture for this day and age: "There is a generation that is pure in its own eyes, yet is not washed from its filthiness" (Proverbs 30:12).

NOT JUST ONE APPLE

It was Epicurus who said, "Is God willing to prevent evil, but not able? Then He is not omnipotent. Is He able, but not willing? Then He is malevolent. Is He both able and willing? Then whence cometh evil? Is He neither able nor willing? Then why call Him God?"

Epicurus seemed to cover every base but the right one. He forgot about something the KJV of the Bible calls "the longsuffering of God." The Scriptures make it clear that God will punish evil, but we have a problem. We don't see ourselves as being evil (see Psalm 36:2, Proverbs 12:15, Proverbs 16:2, Proverbs 21:2). Do you think you are evil? Of course you don't. No one does. We think that we are good people, and by (low) human standards many of us are. However, by God's standards we are evil to the core—and there's not just one bad apple.

Here's God's point of view of humanity:

> As it is written: There is none righteous, no, not one; there is none who understands; there is none who seeks after God. They have all turned aside; they have together become unprofitable; there is none who does good, no, not one. Their throat is an open tomb; with their tongues they have practiced deceit; the poison of asps is under their lips; Whose mouth is full of cursing and bitterness. Their feet are swift to shed blood; destruction and misery are in their ways; and the way of peace they have not known. There is no fear of God before their eyes (Romans 3:10-18).

We are warned many times in Scripture that God is going to judge humanity from the standard of moral perfection (see Matthew 5:27-28), and that will put every one of us justly in Hell. Yet, we are told that this same God of perfect justice is rich in mercy. He is patiently waiting for evil sinners to repent and be forgiven.

So don't mistake the mercy and patience of God for the thought that He's impotent or doesn't care about justice. If you die in your sins there won't be a second chance. Come to your senses, repent, and trust the Savior today. You will have eternity to thank God that you did.

At the beginning of 2009, an atheist named Kat left a comment on "Atheist Central" saying that I was filled with hatred. I asked her if she could possibly find the time to go through each of my blogs and give me some specifics. She said that she would, but I didn't hear back from her and presumed that she hadn't found anything. Three months later she wrote that she had been busy and was still looking.

More recently, she left another comment saying:

> "I gave up collecting all of your mean and rude comments to the atheists who post here; all of the mean and hateful things you've posted, because it simply became too much.... I can't do it anymore Ray, I simply cannot keep going through your archives and finding every instance of your cruelty, it hurts my heart way too much...your hatred, your hateful words, your insults and cruelty, cannot be read by me for even one minute longer. This will be my last comment on your blog. I cannot allow myself to be witness to such cruelty any longer."

Unfortunately Kat didn't provide even one example. If she was speaking the truth and I have been hateful and cruel, please forgive me. I am not aware of any hatred I have for any human being. My motivation is one of love and always has been. I do admit to mocking atheists, because mockery is a legitimate form of debate according to my rule Book. God Himself mocks evil men who refuse His moral government (see Proverbs 1:26-27). The Bible also calls the professing atheist a "fool" (Psalm 14:1, Psalm 107:17, Proverbs 12:15, Proverbs 14:16, Luke 12:20).

So if you do take the time to go through my writing, you will find many incidents of mockery when it comes to the unscientific and ridiculous theory tale of evolution (which I once believed). You will find me speaking of the Bible calling atheists fools, of April 1 being National Atheist Day, etc. Any references I have used to moral corruption, filthiness, wickedness of heart, etc., include myself and the rest of humanity (see Romans 3:11-18) and are from the Scriptures. Any comparisons of humanity to pigs, foxes, dogs, sheep, etc., are biblical metaphors. But I am not aware of any hatred or cruelty.

I think that perhaps Kat is a tender-hearted person who doesn't have the grit to be able to handle healthy debate. May her tender heart be turned toward her Creator.

CHAPTER NINE

WHO KILLED JFK?

"[We are being] told that our atheism is an 'intellectual embarrassment' by a man who actually believes that he's going to literally fly in the air like some kind of bird one fine day: 'For the Lord himself shall descend from heaven with a shout, with the voice of the archangel, and with the trump of God: and the dead in Christ shall rise first: Then we which are alive and remain shall be caught up together with them in the clouds, to meet the Lord in the air: and so shall we ever be with the Lord' (1 Thessalonians 4:16-17). As an atheist I love it when Christians try to lecture me about the logic of atheism!"

IF YOU THINK human beings being able to fly is crazy, think about what this commenter and his fellow unbelievers believe. A staunch atheist believes that there isn't a "creation," that nothing was "designed," neither was it "created" or "made." He also believes that he has no beliefs, because that would mean that he has some sort of "faith," which is another word that has connotations about you-know-Who.

When pressed about his beliefs, the average atheist will admit that he believes that 14.5 billion years ago the universe came into being from something. But he doesn't know what the "something" was, although he is adamant that it wasn't God. Then, through the miracle of evolution, the something that wasn't God brought into being everything we see.

Someone once said that (with all our technology) we have trouble trying to figure out who killed JFK. That was only forty-five or so years ago and 14.5 billion years is a long time to be sure of anything. A mere million years ago is a long time, let alone more than fourteen thousand million years, but that is what's necessary for the miracle of evolution to work. Of course, that figure has been revised a number of times in recent history and no doubt in a hundred years' time science will laugh at what is now believed.

> We have trouble trying to figure out who killed JFK. That was only forty-five or so years ago and 14.5 billion years is a long time to be sure of anything.

I choose rather to call creation "creation," and to love and serve the Creator who bought creation into being. I have no trouble believing that He made man as male and female, and that He gave them the ability to procreate after their own kind. I have no trouble believing that He brought animals to Noah, flooded the earth to the highest mountain, opened the Red Sea, stopped the mouths of Daniel's lions, guided the stone from David's sling, fed the five thousand fresh bread and fish, died on a cruel cross for our sins, and then rose from the dead on the third day.

It's easy to believe in miracles because I see the unspeakable genius of God's handiwork every time I watch a bird fly. It has been one hundred years since we first flew, yet we still can't make a plane land with the agility of the common sparrow. In most modern landings someone is gripping the armrest, and most thank God when they hear the "thud" as we come back to earth.

THE ATHEIST AND FAITH

Banks are built on faith. You trust the bank with your money. Wall Street is built on trust. Marriage is built on trust. If you lose faith in your marriage partner (you don't trust him or her) you have in essence lost your marriage. Friendships are built on trust. If I don't trust you and you don't trust me, then we have no basis for a friendship.

Trust is what holds a doctor-patient relationship together like hyphenations. Trust is what you exercise every time you swallow a pill or receive a booster shot. Faith is there when you allow your dentist to drill and fill. You trust both his ability and his integrity. It's there when you let a surgeon operate or when you let a stranger prepare your food in a restaurant or at a drive-through. You trust that his hands are clean and that the food is fresh.

You have trust when you ride a roller coaster or put on a parachute, when you cross a bridge or fly in a plane. You have faith in your car when you drive it, in the gasoline when you pump it, and when you put on its brakes. You trust the driver on the other side of a yellow line will stay on his side of the road. You have trust when you sit down on a chair, drink a can of Coke, bite into a candy bar, or spread ketchup on hot fries. We have faith in history books, science books, newspapers, and often a misplaced trust in politicians. We even trust elevators, knowing that they can let us down.

Trust me, there are some people who don't know the meaning of trust in God, despite having it written on our currency.

They think that someone who has faith in God "believes" in His existence without a hint of evidence. However, eternal life comes from trusting in the person of Jesus Christ, not simply in a belief in His historical existence. Look at how the Bible differentiates belief from an implicit trust: "But without faith it is impossible to please Him, for he who comes to God must believe that He is [a belief in His existence—clearly evidenced by creation to all but a fool—see Psalm 14:1, Romans 1:20], and that He is a rewarder of those who diligently seek Him (trust)" (Hebrews 11:6).

If a man refused to have trust, he wouldn't cross a bridge, ride an elevator, fly in a plane, go to a doctor, or use a banker. Such a person would live in paranoia. I knew a man like that once. He was an atheist. He was afraid to fly. He was afraid of crowds because he thought someone might try and kill him. He was so paranoid he didn't even use his real name.

May you and I always remember how "trust" is the oxygen of human relationships. It is the oil that makes things work, and it's the means of exchange between God and man.

THE SECURITY BLANKET

It's common for atheists to say, "The world is a big scary place, and when people come to this realization (existential dread if you've heard of Sartre, et. al.), religion is there to act as a security blanket with all of its false promises and 'guarantees.' Personally, I look within when I need to make important decisions, and to family and friends when I need support. You look to a two-thousand-year old work of semi-fiction. Horses for courses I suppose."

Religion *is* a security blanket. All it does is provide a physiological sanctuary. Nothing else. It has caused atrocities throughout history, and still does today. Religious people murdered God's prophets throughout the Old Testament. They stoned Stephen to death for his preaching of the truth (see Acts 7:51-60). They erroneously believe that a man can earn his own salvation through his own religious works. Religion delivers only a security blanket when a parachute is needed. When the "jump" comes, these people will see their terrible error.

However, when someone becomes a Christian (through the new birth of John 3), they are set free from the bondage of religion. This is because God Himself provides a parachute in the Savior (see Ephesians 2:8-9).

The support of friends and family is wonderful. We all need that. But look at how the three-thousand-year-old Word of God describes those of us who leave God out of the equation: "The wicked, through the pride of his countenance, will not seek after God: God is not in all his thoughts. His ways are always grievous; your judgments are far above out of his sight: as for all his enemies, he puffs at them. He has said in his heart, I shall not be moved: for I shall never be in adversity" (Psalm 10:4-6). You have an enemy that came to kill, steal and destroy (see John 10:10). You may make it through this life without the mercy of God, but it is for the next that you need a Savior.

CONFUSED ATHEIST

Another popular argument is to apply Old Testament laws to contemporary life: "I have violated some of the strictures in the Bible. I work on Sunday, I wear cotton polyester blend T shirts sometimes, I love lobster, when my children disobey I choose to let them live, I don't own any slaves. Lots of things like that so I have violated your Bible but that is not God's law because there is no God to make laws. Just an old book of barbarian myths."

You are a little confused about the Law that will judge you. The complete Hebrew Law has a total of 613 precepts. It is broken into three categories:

1. *The Ceremonial Law.* For the worship of God—how the Tabernacle was to be constructed, what to wear—ordinances saying not to wear cotton and wool together because the combination produces sweat. What to eat—certain animals are "scavengers" and are not healthy to eat, etc.

2. *The Civil Law.* How the nation of Israel was to govern. How they were to treat their slaves (servants), how they were to punish murderers and rapists, how to stop rebellion, etc.

3. *The Moral Law.* The Ten Commandments. God sees the thought life of each of us and considers lust a violation of the Seventh Commandment (see Matthew 5:27-28). He also sees hatred as murder. It is the Moral Law that you are bound by (see Romans 2:15) and that is the Law that will judge you on Judgment Day (see Romans 2:12, James 2:12). It is the Moral Law that will justly send you to Hell for your sins.

However, God in His great kindness offers you forgiveness of sins through repentance and faith in Jesus—everlasting life. Only a fool would refuse such an incredible offer. Please think about your salvation. There's nothing more important than where you will spend eternity.

Listen to this argument given by someone who calls himself "Happy Humanist." He said, "So how do you explain the verses in Matthew 10:34-35 where Jesus says that 'Think not that I am come to send peace on earth: I came not to send peace, but a sword. For I am come to set a man against his father and the daughter against her mother and the daughter-in-law against her mother-in-law.' How does this square with 'honor your father and mother' in the Ten Commandments?'"

If a Mafia boss reforms and becomes a police officer then returns to his criminal friends and tells them that they should stop their life of crime because there is going to be a big bust, he's not going to be Mr. Popular. Some may listen to him, but the majority are going to see him as a threat to their lucrative means of livelihood. They will hate him and may even kill him. They don't hate him personally, but the badge for which he stands. They hate the law and anyone who seeks to uphold it.

The Christian is nothing but a criminal who has turned from his sins and seeks to warn his fellow criminals that there is going to be a big bust. Judgment Day is coming. Jesus warned His followers that they would be hated because they belonged to Him. He warned that people would kill them, thinking that they were doing God a favor. This happened during history, and especially during the Spanish Inquisition, when the Catholic Church (in the name of God) tortured and killed Christians:

> The Inquisition, which the Catholic sovereigns had been empowered to establish by Sixtus IV in 1478, had, despite unjustifiable cruelties, failed of its purpose, chiefly for want of centralisation. In 1483 the pope appointed Torquemada, who had been an assistant inquisitor since 11 February 1482, Grand Inquisitor of Castile, and on 17 October extended his jurisdiction over Aragon."[1]

Jesus said that the world would hate Him because He testified of their deeds, that they were evil. This is why I keep saying that the issue with the atheist isn't intellectual, it is moral. It's not that the atheist "can't" find God. It's that he "won't" (see Psalm 10:4), because he loves the darkness and hates the light (see John 3:19-20). The professing atheist sees Christianity as a threat to his pleasure-filled and sinful lifestyle. The book of Romans says that his "carnal mind" (the rebellious mind of man) is in a place of hostility toward God. Then Scripture pinpoints where the hostility is directed—at the Moral Law (see Romans 8:7). Sinful man hates the Law of God. That's why it's easy for me to love those who mock and hate me. It's because I know that they don't hate me personally but what I stand for—I wear the badge of the Moral Law.

It is this hatred for God and His Law that brings a "sword" (division and hostility) between the Christian and this sinful world. This sharp sword of separation even happens in families. Almost every Christian I know has experienced this. But the greatest way I can love and honor my parents is to tell them how to avoid the reality of Hell and find everlasting life that is alone in Jesus Christ.

We broke God's Law. Jesus paid our fine. That means that God can legally dismiss our case and give us everlasting life. What is unbelievable is anyone refusing such an incredible gift.

We are fortunate that in this country the sword that comes between us and our families is merely figurative. In some Islamic countries if a family member becomes a Christian, the family sees it as their God-given duty to put him to death in an "honor" killing.

The time may come when that sword will turn toward the Christian in the United States as the country becomes more godless and consequently hate-filled toward God. This is because resistance to abortion, gambling, drinking, pornography, gay marriage, drug legalization, fornication, etc., comes mainly from the Christian community. We are a very real threat to the world's lucrative lawlessness. If that day comes, may God give us the courage to love not our lives unto death. After all, we are fighting the "good" fight of faith, and this sinful world can't kill a soldier of Christ. It can merely promote him to Headquarters.

AN ATHEIST'S QUESTION ABOUT THE CROSS

"[God] sacrificed Himself to Himself so that he would not violate His perception of justice. He gets mad when we don't accept His sacrifice of Himself to Himself. This sounds believable to people?"

Let's put it differently so that it sounds believable. God is just and holy. That means that He is a like a good judge who sees a devious criminal who has viciously murdered eight innocent young girls. If the judge is good, he is going to be mad at the criminal and throw the book at him. That makes sense.

God is extremely mad at sinners (see Romans 2:5-6), and because He is good the Day is coming when He will throw the Book at every criminal who has violated His Law. Yet this same wrath-filled judge is rich in mercy and became a human being in Jesus of Nazareth so that we could be forgiven. We broke God's Law. Jesus paid our fine. That means that God can *legally* dismiss our case and give us everlasting life. That makes it believable.

What is unbelievable is anyone refusing such an incredible gift.

HATING PARENTS, ETC.

"Ray, You say that '[God] also warns that if you hate someone, you have as good as killed them.' Then why does Jesus proclaim the following? 'If anyone comes to Me and does not hate his father and mother, wife and children, brothers and sisters, yes, and his own life also, he cannot be My disciple' (Luke 14:26). So to be a Christian you have to be both homicidal and suicidal. If you're not, then you're not a disciple of Christ. I welcome a thorough explanation of this conundrum."

This is what is known as "hyperbole." It's a statement of exaggeration, contrasting love with hate for the sake of emphasis. We still use hyperbole in everyday speech—"I have told you a million times not to exaggerate." The Bible often uses hyperbole to make a point. The Book of Proverbs says that if you fail to discipline your child you "hate" him. The obvious point is that discipline is a token of parental love.

Luke 14:26 shows that Jesus of Nazareth was either a deluded raving lunatic (which doesn't match the brilliance of His other words—read the Sermon on the Mount given to us in Matthew 5:7) or He was God in human form. He is saying that we should so love Him that our love for our mother, father, etc., (our "loved" ones) should seem like hate compared to the love we have for the One who gave us those loved ones in the first place. This is the essence of the first of the Ten Commandments.

> "But let me ask you this. Do you really feel so much love for Jesus that it feels like you hate everyone else by comparison?"

Remember the reason for hyperbole. It is to give us contrast. I don't "hate" anyone. I deeply love my siblings, my wonderful wife, my three kids, my grandchildren, and my parents. However, love for God is much deeper, and there's good reason for that. My parents didn't give me life. God did. He also gave me my wife, my brother and sister, my children, the ability to see, to think and hear, to love, to eat, and to breathe. To love the gift above the Giver of those gifts is called "inordinate" affection. It is a form of idolatry. It's only right that I love the One who lavished these incredible blessings on me. However, this same gracious and kind Creator went even further. He became a human being in the person of Jesus of Nazareth and took the punishment for my many sins. He did this so that I could legally have my death sentence commuted and be granted the gift of everlasting life. What sort of wretched person would I be if I didn't return such love with every ounce of my being? Don't you love God for His kindness to you? See 1 Corinthians 16:22.

HISTORY'S BIGGEST EVENT

What do you think was the most significant event in human history?

Unquestionably, the greatest event was the faint sound of a heartbeat in a cold and lifeless body in a tomb two thousand years ago. The sound of blood rushing through the heart of Jesus of Nazareth was a sound that will thunder throughout eternity because of its incredible implications.

The fact that God raised someone from the dead is not really significant. Stories of His raising the dead appear a number of times in both the Old and New Testaments. But this resurrection had enormous legal repercussions. It was evidence that the Judge of the universe had acknowledged that the payment for our sins was acceptable. It was the key that unlocked the door to immortality for humanity.

Here's another question for you. What is the most precious substance in the universe? It was unquestionably the blood of Jesus Christ. Nothing else could redeem us from the just curse of God's Law. When eternal justice called for our blood, Jesus gave His blood to atone for our crimes. We were not redeemed with silver and gold…but with the precious blood of Christ.

Many Jews had been crucified as criminals on the Roman cross. All suffered unspeakable pain. But this Jew's suffering was different because He was the Lamb of God, whose blood did not contain the taint of sin carried by the lineage of Adam. He was truly the Lamb of God.

These are wonderful biblical truths that Christians know and rejoice in. But, during Easter, millions of both Jews and Gentiles celebrate biblical events that they don't fully understand. For one or two holy days they give God thanks for His mercy and for the Passover lamb. Christians celebrate Easter and the resurrection of the Passover Lamb every day of the year.

CHAPTER TEN

THE MIRROR

I T IS HUMAN nature to shed personal blame for our sins. Take for instance these words: "It is strange that you believe God created a set of rules that we are supposed to live by and created these rules and we humans in such a way that none of us can follow them. We all sin. When we sin God blames us for following our nature and being incapable of living sin free."

But that won't hold water on Judgment Day. It wouldn't even work in civil court: "Judge, society's rules are too hard to keep, and you are trying to blame me when it's merely my nature to violate the law."

Let's ask the question as to which of God's "rules" is unfair? Is it the one that says it's wrong to lie? Steal? Murder? Commit adultery? Perhaps it's the one that says that we should love Him above all things. But the First Commandment is reasonable. God gave us life and every blessing we enjoy. All the rules do is what the mirror does for us each morning. It shows us that we need to go to the water and wash. It reflects the truth. The mirror of God's Law shows us that we are ungrateful, sin-loving sinners who desperately need to be washed from the uncleanliness of our sins. And that was the purpose of the Cross. Jesus took the punishment for our sins so that we could be morally clean on the Day of Judgment.

Someone e-mailed me and said that I teach "that lust in the heart is a sin. Lust is a biological impulse, not a freely chosen activity." Before we look at the issue of whether or not lust is a sin, let's define the word. Lust is "unlawful" desire. It is not to be confused with the sex drive. God gave us the pleasures of sex, but it came with an instruction Book. The Bible tells us that it is to be confined to the institution of marriage. That's the rule. All around us we see privileges that come with rules. If you have the privilege of driving a vehicle, the rule in the United States is that you stay to the right side of the road. Drive on the left and you will cause big problems. Think of the marriages that have been destroyed because the rules were broken. Think of the STDs that plague humanity because the rules were broken.

Adultery begins in the mind. It is an unlawful desire. The thought precedes the deed, and God Himself says that if you desire to commit adultery you have as much as done the deed. He also warns that if you hate someone, you have as good as killed them.

The Scriptures tell us that we share our thought life with the One who gave us a brain. He sees what He created, and He destroyed an entire generation "because the imagination of their heart was continually evil." So pleading that you couldn't help lusting will not exonerate you from moral responsibility and its terrible eternal consequences. However, repentance and faith in Jesus will.

WHO IS THE PAINTER?

"Ray, when you see a painting, it is reasonable to assume that a painter painted it. Is it reasonable to assume that his name is Alan Jeffrey Pinkerton? How would you go about validating your claim? Would it be enough for you if someone just told you his name was Alan Jeffrey Pinkerton? What if somebody else told you that Alan Jeffrey Pinkerton never existed and it was really painted by Cecil P. Fitzwilliam? Imagine that it is your job to find out who really painted it. How would you begin your investigation? You see, creation equals creator is all well and good...but how do I establish who that creator was?"

In other words, it is obvious that there is a God, but what is His identity? Moses asked the same question on Mount Sinai.

The One who created the universe must be supernatural. With all our "genius," humanity can't create one grain of sand, a leaf, a flower or a bird, from nothing. The Creator must have powers that are infinitely greater than those of the greatest human being. The claim of the Gospel is that this Creator will reveal Himself to all who repent and trust Jesus Christ.

This isn't a reference to a change of belief or a change of religious philosophy. It's the supernatural experience of being born again. It was radical for me to be born the first time (natural birth). I didn't exist, then (in a matter of nine months) I was breathing the earth's air. The second birth (supernatural birth) I had on April 25th, 1972, was just as radical as the first. Only the Creator could do that. It was through the cross that I was able to understand God's love for me.

How can you demonstrate that you love someone? You could buy that person an expensive ring. I'm sure that would help, because it's tangible evidence of a sacrifice. Still, it comes back to belief. If the person you love chooses not to believe that you love them, there's nothing you can do about it.

I was in New Zealand early in 2009, at a university where local Christians had organized a debate between me and an atheist. Just before it started a tall outspoken man named Ryan enthusiastically approached me and said something like, "I'm honored to meet you. I have watched your videos on the Internet, read your material, and here I am actually getting to meet you. I am really excited about this debate." As he was walking back to his seat I called out, "Which side are you on?" and he replied, "I'm against *everything* you stand for."

During the question time Ryan asked some good questions. The next day he showed up at another meeting at which I was speaking, then he listened to me again, for another hour or so at a church service. Afterward we chatted. I signed a book for him, we had our photo taken, and he even helped at the book table. I really cared about Ryan and was pleased to hear him say at the end of the evening, "Man, why are you so likeable!!!" The fact that he could feel my love and concern for him was more powerful than any argument I could give him for the existence of God.

Some atheists read everything I write as if I write in hatred. Yet I love and care about you. If I could have lunch with you, I would, and I would gladly pay the tab. But if you refuse to believe that, I can't do anything about it.

You accuse me of making money from the sale of my books, but did you know that I have preached open air more than five thousand times and never been paid? I do that because I love people and care where they spend eternity. If I didn't care, I wouldn't bother with preaching, blogging, producing a TV program, or writing Christian books. I had a very successful business before I became a Christian and could have made a good living, but I chose to spend my life pleading with people like you to consider where you will spend eternity.

So think about my motive and then please think of God's motive for the Cross: "But God shows and clearly proves His [own] love for us by the fact that while we were still sinners, Christ (the

Messiah, the Anointed One) died for us" (Romans 5:8, *Amplified Bible*). That's the ultimate sacrifice. It's up to you to believe it.

Sir Isaac Newton said:

> Atheism is so senseless and odious to mankind that it never had many professors. Can it be by accident that all birds, beasts, and men have their right side and left side alike shaped…and just two eyes and no more on either side of the face and just two ears on either side of the head and a nose with two holes and no more between the eyes and one mouth under the nose…These and such like considerations always have and ever will prevail with mankind to believe that there is a Being who made all things and has all things in his power and who is therefore to be feared.

DARWIN'S CABBAGE RACISM

Charles Darwin's *Origin of Species* hasn't always had that title. The book's full title is *On the Origin of Species by Means of Natural Selection, or the Preservation of Favoured Races in the Struggle for Life*. For some reason, in the sixth edition of 1872 the title was changed. Deborah Drapper said, "Yes its title really is a bit too long. So why don't we call it *The Preservation of Favoured Races*? Don't you think it is time to give the other half of the title its turn? It might catch on really well."

Of course Darwin's followers don't think he was a racist. When he was talking about "favored races," he wasn't talking about people, but cabbages:

> Nevertheless, as our varieties certainly do occasionally revert in some of their characters to ancestral forms, it seems to me not improbable, that if we could succeed in naturaliz-ing, or were to cultivate, during many generations, the sev-

eral races, for instance, of the cabbage, in very poor soil (in which case, however, some effect would have to be attributed to the direct action of the poor soil), that they would to a large extent, or even wholly, revert to the wild aboriginal stock.[1]

However, before faithful believers stand in line to look at the facial hair of Charles Darwin in England's Natural History Museum, they may want to rethink the character of the man to whom they are paying homage. Darwin also said:

> Lastly, more than one writer has asked, why have some animals had their mental powers more highly developed than others, as such development would be advantageous to all? Why have not apes acquired the intellectual powers of man? Various causes could be assigned; but as they are conjectural, and their relative probability cannot be weighed, it would be useless to give them. A definite answer to the latter question ought not to be expected, seeing that no one can solve the simpler problem why, of two races of savages, one has risen higher in the scale of civilization than the other; and this apparently implies increased brain-power."[2]

When Adam and Eve rebelled against God, He cursed them and the earth, and we now live in what is commonly called a "fallen creation."

At some future period, not very distant as measured by centuries, the civilized races of man will almost certainly exterminate and replace throughout the world the savage races. At the same time the anthropomorphous apes, as Professor Schaaffhausen has remarked, will no doubt be exterminated. The break will then be rendered wider, for it will intervene between man in a more civilized state, as we may hope, than the Caucasian, and some ape as low as a baboon, instead of as at present between the negro or Australian and the gorilla."[3]

How do atheists justify the fact the Charles Darwin was a racist? They say, "Darwin himself was far less racist than most of his contemporaries."[4]

When I once mentioned that I had had the flu, an atheist wrote and said, "Sorry to hear that you're unwell. I just wonder why are you sick? I mean, really. Your irreducibly complex immune system obviously isn't complex enough to handle the flu, and we all know there's no evolution to make the virus evolve. Did God create the flu? Is it then part of His 'mysterious ways'? I'm actually interested in your answer here (for once, I might add), because you often talk about the big things but rarely about the everyday things. What glorious explanation do you have for the flu?"

When God made Adam and Eve He made them perfect. There was no disease, suffering, pain, or death. When they rebelled against Him, He cursed them and the earth, and we now live in what is commonly called a "fallen creation."

Study the soil for a moment. It naturally produces weeds. No one plants them, no one waters them. They even stubbornly push through cracks of a dry sidewalk. Billions of useless weeds sprout like there's no tomorrow, strangling our crops and ruining our lawns. Pull them out by the roots, and there will be more tomorrow. They are nothing but a curse.

Consider how much of the earth is uninhabitable. There are millions of square miles of barren deserts in Africa and other parts of the world. Most of Australia is nothing but miles and miles of useless desolate land. Not only that, but the earth is constantly shaken with massive earthquakes. Its shores are lashed with hurricanes, tornadoes rip through creation with incredible fury, devastating floods soak the land, and terrible droughts parch the soil. Sharks, tigers, lions, snakes, spiders, and disease-carrying mosquitoes attack humanity and suck its lifeblood. The earth's inhabitants are afflicted with disease, pain, suffering, and death.

Think of how many people are plagued with cancer, Alzheimer's, multiple sclerosis, heart disease, emphysema, Parkinson's, and a number of other debilitating illnesses. Consider all the children with leukemia, or people born with crippling diseases or without the mental capability to even feed themselves. All these things should convince thinking minds that something is radically wrong. Did God mess up when He created humanity? What sort of tyrant must our Creator be if this was His master plan? Sadly, many use the issue of suffering as an excuse to reject any thought of God, when its existence is the very reason we should accept Him. Suffering stands as terrible testimony to the truth of the explanation given by the Word of God.

But how can we know that the Bible is true? Simply by studying the prophecies of Matthew 24, Luke 21, and 2 Timothy 3. A few minutes of open-hearted inspection will convince any honest skeptic that this is no ordinary book. It is the supernatural testament of our Creator about why there is suffering…and what we can do about it. The Bible tells us that God cursed the earth because of Adam's transgression. Weeds are a curse. So are flu and all other diseases. Sin and suffering cannot be separated. Again, the Scriptures inform us that we live in a fallen creation. In the beginning, God created man perfect, and he lived in a perfect world without suffering. It was heaven on earth. When sin came into the world, death and misery came with it. Those who understand the message of Holy Scripture eagerly await a new heaven and a new earth "wherein dwells righteousness." In that coming Kingdom there will be no more pain, suffering, disease, or death. We are told that no eye has ever seen, nor has any ear heard, neither has any man's mind ever imagined the wonderful things that God has in store for those who love Him (1 Corinthians 2:9). Think for a moment what it would be like if food grew with the fervor of weeds. Consider how wonderful it would be if the deserts became incredibly fertile, if creation stopped devouring humanity. Imagine if the weather worked for us instead of against us, if disease completely disappeared, if pain were a thing of the past, if death were no more.

The dilemma is that we are like a child whose insatiable appetite for chocolate has caused his face to break out with ugly sores. He looks in the mirror and sees a sight that makes him depressed. But instead of giving up his beloved chocolate, he consoles himself by stuffing more into his mouth. Yet the source of his pleasure is actually the cause of his suffering. The whole face of the earth is nothing but ugly sores of suffering. Everywhere we look we see unspeakable pain. But instead of believing God's explanation and asking Him to forgive us and change our appetite, we run deeper into sin's sweet embrace. There we find solace in its temporal pleasures, thus intensifying our pain both in this life and in the life to come.

CHAPTER ELEVEN

THE SUBJECT OF LYING

"Ray is flat-out lying to you."
"I'm sick of your constant lying, Ray."
"You're a dishonest, lying for Jesus, punk."
"Lying for Jesus again?"
"That makes you a liar Ray."
"You liar, Ray!"
"So I repeat. Ray is lying. Lying is wrong."
"You are an ignorant, lying idiot."
"You are a liar. If your God exists, he will condemn
you to hell."

T HE ABOVE comments where made by atheists. I would like them to explain why it's wrong to lie and from where does an atheist get this moral code by which he judges right from wrong? If he believes that it's shaped by society, if society says that lying is okay (91 percent of Americans lie regularly), is it then right? The point is that each of us has a God-given conscience that intuitively tells us that lying is morally wrong.

This is how an atheist handles the subject:

"Lying is wrong (in nearly all situations). But not because the Bible says so….For example, 'I threw a ball into the sky, and it never came down.' Well that's a lie because we know the truth of gravity; the ball had to come back down if you merely threw it. To speak such a lie is evil because it is irrational—it makes no sense to claim the ball never came down."

What say a bird flew off with the ball in its big mouth? How about a low flying plane sucked it into its engine, or lightning hit it and it disintegrated?

Don't be so quick to call the ball-throwing man a liar and "evil," when you simply haven't thought the issue through very thoroughly. If you do that, you are the one who is irrational.

If an atheist believes that there is no God and that there are no moral absolutes, then there is nothing morally wrong with lying. Instead, it comes down to what works best for each of us. It's an issue of convenience rather than one of morality.

What's then with the continual accusations of lying, as if I were doing something morally wrong? They are meaningless if there is no God, as you say you believe.

So, here are your two choices. 1. If you are right and there's no God, my misrepresenting your beliefs (my so-called "lying") is simply how I survive as part of this evolving species. 2. If I am right and there is a God, and I am guilty of lying, it will result in me being damned in Hell. Which one would you like to be true?

Another atheist weighs in: "Who was the atheist who said 'lying is wrong?' I didn't get his/her name. Anyway, there is no right or wrong in the natural world. However, there are things that are a good idea while other things are bad ideas. That is not 'good' or 'bad' in the moral sense, but 'good' or 'bad' in the sense that if it's a bad idea it might get you into some type of trouble, while a good idea might keep you out of trouble."

You did the right thing to call that atheist out on the admission that lying is wrong. He let the cat out of the bag. But in your effect to put the feline back in, you put yourself onto a slippery slope.

So you think that there is no right or wrong? There are just good ideas and bad ideas. Do you remember little Jessica Lunsford? She was the nine-year-old girl kidnapped from her home in Homosassa, Florida, in the early morning of February 24, 2005. She was raped and later buried alive (clutching her teddy bear) by forty-seven-year-old John Couey, who was living nearby. Nothing wrong there. Just a bad idea. I wonder why the judge gave him the death sentence.

Six million Jews gassed to death by Nazis. Bad idea, depending on your perspective. There were two hundred thousand people murdered in the United States in the 1990s. A lot of bad ideas. Never mind. Nothing wrong done there.

This good idea/bad idea philosophy sure is going to save our country a lot of time and money in the future, because there will be no need for court systems, judges, lawyers, and prisons because there's no right or wrong, just good ideas and bad ideas. And you can't prosecute someone for having a bad idea.

The Bible says: "For the wrath of God is revealed from heaven against all ungodliness and unrighteousness of men, who suppress the truth in unrighteousness..." The Scriptures tell us that the issue with the atheist is moral. He maintains that it is intellectual, but the Bible makes it clear that he is offended by the thought of God's moral government (see Romans 8:7). He knows intuitively that every one of the Ten Commandments is right, but he suppresses that knowledge, and in doing so, calls for God's just wrath to abide on him (see John 3:36): "[B]ecause what may be known of God is manifest in them [via the conscience], for God has shown it to them."

This is how God has shown it to them: "For since the creation of the world His invisible attributes are clearly seen, being understood by the things that are made, even His eternal power and Godhead, so that they are without excuse…"

The professing atheist is without excuse—because creation reveals that there is a Creator. He doesn't need anything else. He doesn't need to have the Bible proven to be the Word of God, or see a miracle, or have God appear in front of him. It is because of this inbuilt understanding that he will be without excuse on Judgment Day. Then the Scriptures give more reasons for the atheist's just damnation:

[B]ecause, although they knew God [through creation and the conscience], they did not glorify Him as God [they refuse to give God due praise for life itself, and for this incredible creation in which we live], nor were thankful [the sin of ingratitude], but became futile in their thoughts [*The Amplified Bible* brings out the original Greek language— "But instead they became futile and godless in their thinking with vain imaginings, foolish reasoning, and stupid speculations and their senseless minds were darkened." Wow, what a perfect description of the stupid speculations of Darwinian evolution, blindly embracing an unsubstantiated, unscientific fairy tale for grownups, because they foolishly think that it deals with the moral dilemma of having to face God], and their foolish hearts were darkened. Professing to be wise, they became fools [Another amazingly perfect description of the atheistic evolutionist. He embraces an imaginary theory that came from the over-fertile mind of a man bitter at God because of the loss of his beloved daughter. And so the atheist calls all who don't believe as he does an unscientific knuckle-dragger], and changed the glory of the incorruptible God into an image made like corruptible man—and birds and four-footed animals and creeping things.

So if you are a professing atheist, please rethink your beliefs. God doesn't go away just because you don't believe in Him. You have to face Him on Judgment Day and you desperately need a Savior.

Most contemporary atheists carefully say that they "lack belief in gods." I say "carefully" because they don't want to be seen as having any "faith" at all, probably because of its overtones.

So let's look closely at what they are saying. If I tell you "I lack belief that my Ford truck has a maker," I am saying that I think nothing made it. It just happened. That is scientifically impossible. Nothing is nothing. It cannot "make" anything. If it can make something, then it's not nothing because it has the power to make something.

> If you are a professing atheist, please rethink your beliefs. God doesn't go away just because you don't believe in Him. You have to face Him on Judgment Day and you desperately need a Savior.

So the contemporary atheist with his semantics paints himself into an intellectual dilemma. He has the choice of thinking nothing made everything, that something made everything (perhaps God) and is no longer an atheist, or he joins the "Don't Understand How" club—the DUH.

Penn Jillette is a well-known atheist. Look at his honesty when it comes to the issue of believing: "I believe that there is no God. I'm beyond atheism. Atheism is not believing in God. Not believing in God is easy....But, this 'This I Believe' thing seems to demand something more personal, some leap of faith that helps one see life's big picture, some rules to live by. So, I'm saying, 'This I believe: I believe there is no God.'"

I had to smile the other day. I looked up the word *Homo sapien*. This is what it said: "A human being, also human or man, is a member of a species of bipedal primates in the family *Homo sapiens*—Latin: "wise human" or "knowing human")....Humans have a highly developed brain."

Man believes that he is related to primates and in the same breath he describes himself as having a highly developed brain. "Highly developed" is a relative term. Compared to what? Can a man catch a Frisbee in his mouth six feet off the ground? Can he single-handedly round up a thousand sheep, sniff out illegal drugs hidden deep within a suitcase, or hear the faintest sound of a burglar open a door in the early hours of the morning? Can he fly with the agility of a sparrow?

Do you think that you are a wise human with a highly developed brain? Are you the master of your own destiny and therefore in complete control? Then let me remind you that you are not. You have no control over your breathing. Your lungs start and stop irrespective of your will. So does your blinking, and your swallowing. You can't stop yourself from sleeping or even from dreaming. You probably couldn't even stop a hiccup, a sneeze, or a yawn...if your life depended on it. Even the mention of the word "yawn" is probably setting you off on one right now. Yawn. Think of it.

Your heart, liver, pancreas, gallbladder, etc., all function irrespective of your will. You don't even have complete control over your daily bodily functions. You *have* to go. You can't even stop yourself from thinking. Try it. Think of nothing. Bet you can't. Your subconscious voice talks to you incessantly, whether you want it to or not.

We are not the ones who are in control. God is. He gave us life and set us in motion as human beings, and He is the One who says when our number is up. So stop professing yourself to be wise, and instead do what the Bible says: "Let no one deceive himself. If anyone among you seems to be wise in this age, let him become a fool that he may become wise" (1 Corinthians 3:18).

The wonderful irony is that the Bible compares man to a helpless worm (see Job 25:5-6), and yet at the same time says that this helpless worm is of great value to God simply because God is love. This value was revealed once and for all by the fact that our Creator became a lowly human being and gave His life on the Cross so that we could be forgiven our sins and granted the gift of eternal life. So be a wise human—see the New Testament for details.

A LONG-STANDING FRIEND

I have a friend who is seven feet tall. His name is Gilbert. He has big feet. Really big. He wears a size 17 boot—a small canoe for my entire family. I wear a mere 8½.

Gilbert has a big skull, big hands, big bones, and a big brain. You could call him "Homo Great Dane-ian," and me "Homo Chihuahua," if you wish. But whatever you call us, it wouldn't change the fact that we are of the same species—Homo sapiens. Both of us are part of the human family.

There are millions of variations in the fossil record. There are small dinosaurs and there are big dinosaurs. Some have big feet, big skulls, and big bones. There are small dogs and big dogs, big and small horses, and big and small cats. There are bones of birds that had large heads and large claws. There is no argument there. But that's not evidence of Darwinian evolution, just as there is no evolutionary change between Gilbert and myself. We are simply differing forms of the same species. Evolution's believers are still looking for species-to-species transitional forms in the fossil record. There is nothing in the bone record that is empirical evidence of one species transitioning into another species. There are the old bones of a bird that scientists theorize could have been a dinosaur, simply because it has large claws (*Archaeopteryx*). Some modern birds also have claws on their wings, and yet no one claims they are missing links. But they are just "theorizing." They are merely imagining. Like John Lennon. It's easy if you try. Evolutionary "scientists" are good at imagining. They do it with fish, birds, lizards, and of course, humans. They even draw little pictures to make them look real, like the talented Disney imagineers. But it's not reality. In reality, the missing links are still missing.

CHILDREN AND THEIR PROPENSITY TO DO WRONG

"Ray said '[W]e are criminals in God's eyes, who have seriously violated His Law.' Whoa! This is gold, Ray, pure gold! So every newborn baby who has just taken their first breath is a criminal in the eyes of your God? That seems a rather harsh and uncompromising view of things. We bring children into the world so they can be sinners. With a view of the world like this, why would anyone ever want to have children?"

Your "With a view of the world like this, why would anyone ever want to have children?" is interesting. People who believe in the reality of a sinful nature are the ones that have large families, and people who think that man is basically good are the ones that kill their own kids through abortion. So your conclusion is erroneous. A famous preacher once said, "Children without sin?

You without eyes, you mean!" How true. Anyone with kids and who can see will know that children don't have to be taught how to do wrong. They know how to lie and how to be selfish. It comes naturally. That's because they are born with a sinful nature. This isn't harsh or an uncompromising view of life. It's reality. Parents have to teach their children to tell the truth and to share. Leave any child without instruction as to what is right and what is wrong, and he will almost always end up in big trouble.

Popular comedian George Carlin said, "But He loves you. He loves you, and He needs money! He always needs money! He's all-powerful, all-perfect, all-knowing, and all-wise, somehow just can't handle money! Religion takes in billions of dollars, they pay no taxes, and they always need a little more. Now, you talk about a good [expletive] story. [Expletive] [expletive]!"

Despite the fact that most people consider themselves to be morally "good" at heart, the Bible teaches that the heart of man is not good at all. Not in the slightest. It doesn't even teach that he's bad. Its moral prognosis is worse. The Scriptures say that all humanity is desperately wicked to the core. There's not just one bad apple in the barrel.

As Mr. Carlin noticed, this rotten corruption seeps into every area of society. Millions have got away with billions through fraudulent business practices. Many are not only guilty of financial corruption, but men like Stalin and Hitler have murdered millions throughout history using political power. And wicked mankind has also used religion for his own evil purposes. He has not only slaughtered in the name of God, but he's lined his pockets throughout history, and he has done it in more modern times through the medium of television.

Look at how specific the Bible is when it speaks of these money-hungry Bible teachers that will deceive many with their slick words and in so doing slur the name of Christianity: "Many will follow their evil teaching and shameful immorality. And because of these teachers, the way of truth will be slandered. In their greed they will make up clever lies to get hold of your money. But God condemned them long ago, and their destruction will not be delayed" (2 Peter 2:2-3). As the Bible says in this verse, there's good news for the late George Carlin and others like him deeply offended by hypocrisy in religion. All those who have committed any immoral practices (including religious hypocrisy) will end up getting exactly what they deserve. They will be damned in Hell by the justice of Almighty God. No one will get away with a thing. No one.

Years ago I e-mailed the world's most amazing atheist. No, it wasn't Richard Dawkins. Let me give you a clue as to his identity. He was an ordained minister for nineteen years, and during that time he even wrote songs about Jesus, from which he still receives royalties today.

I upset him to a point where he said that if I ever made contact with him again, he would have my e-mail account shut down. He was *really* mad.

I can't tell you his name because he is lawsuit-crazy, but I can tell you what I said to him. All I wrote was, "Judas lasted three and a half years. Yet you managed to fake it for nineteen years! Amazing."

Most professing atheists complain about the Church being full of hypocrites. There *are* millions of hypocrites sitting right in the middle of God's people. They are *pretenders*, whose lives don't match what they profess. Some remain within the Church, while others move on to other things (some to atheism).

But that's the missing link with false converts (hypocrites). They don't know the Lord because they are strangers to true repentance. They hold onto their sins and think that they are Christians when they are not. They are fakes.

Jesus called the ones who stay "goats" among the sheep, and said that they will be sorted out on Judgment Day (see Matthew 7:21-27).

My lawsuit-happy friend played the hypocrite for an incredible nineteen years. No doubt at the time he thought he knew the Lord, just like Judas. But Mr. Iscariot had no idea who Jesus of Nazareth was, evidenced in the fact that he also saw Jesus as simply a means of making money. No doubt today he's still being paid for what he did.

Some would say that this atheist's bark is worse than his bite. I don't think so. He is more than just a barker. He is an angry and bitter man who hates the God he once professed to love. Amazing and yet tragic. This poor man obviously never understood the Cross.

CHAPTER TWELVE

THE MISSING LINK FINALLY FOUND

C REATIONISTS WHO say that there is no proof of Darwinian evolution have been called liars for years:

> Creationists claim there are no transitional fossils, aka missing links. Biologists and paleontologists, among others, know this claim is false…but the fossil record—which is far from complete—is full of them nonetheless, as documented by Occidental College geologist Donald Prothero in his book *Evolution: What the Fossils Say and Why It Matters* (Columbia University Press, 2007)."[1]

So the claim that there are no species-to-species transition forms in the fossil record "is false." Instead evolutionists say that fossil record "is full of them." But look at this May 20, 2009 report about how they had *finally found* the missing link:[2]

> Scientists Unveil Missing Link in Evolution: Scientists have unveiled a 47-million-year-old fossilised skeleton of a monkey hailed as the missing link in human evolution. This 95%-complete "lemur monkey" is described as the "eighth wonder of the world." The search for a direct connection

between humans and the rest of the animal kingdom has taken 200 years—but it was presented to the world today at a special news conference in New York. The discovery of the 95%-complete "lemur monkey"—dubbed Ida—is described by experts as the "eighth wonder of the world." They say its impact on the world of palaeontology will be "somewhat like an asteroid falling down to Earth." Researchers say proof of this transitional species finally confirms Charles Darwin's theory of evolution, and the then radical, outlandish ideas he came up with during his time aboard the *Beagle*. Sir David Attenborough said Darwin "would have been thrilled" to have seen the fossil—and says it tells us who we are and where we came from. "This is the one that connects us directly with them....Now people can say "okay we are primates, show us the link....The link they would have said up to now is missing—well it's no longer missing."

For years we have been told by believers that the theory of evolution is a scientifically proven fact. But this article says that prior to this discovery they had no proof. With this discovery they now believe that "the link they would have said up to now is missing—well it's no longer missing." All this proves is that some scientists are willing to lie to prove their pet theories.

Is this the missing link? Is Ida proof of Darwinism? Not according to CBS news. They said, "*So while we don't know exactly what Ida means to human origins*, she's proof we are endlessly fascinated by where we came from."[3] According to the *Wall Street Journal*, "The discovery has little bearing on a separate paleontological debate centering on the identity of a common ancestor of chimps and humans, which could have lived about six million years ago and still hasn't been found."[4]

The missing link is still missing. So much for the "eighth wonder of the world" and the "asteroid falling down on the world."

Believers in the theory of evolution still have to keep blindly believing without proof. Maybe one day…

When I asked believers in evolution to tell me, in a hundred words or less, what it was that convinced them that it was a scientific fact, someone came back with an impressive:

> Natural selection. Mesonychids, Pakicetus, Ambulocetus, Dalanistes, Rodhocetus, Takracetus, Gaviocetus, Dorudon, Basilosaurus, Mysticetes, Odontocetes. Australopithicus, tiktaalik, burgess shale, archaeopteryx, DNA, mitochondrial DNA, ring species, geographic distribution of animals, the species unique to the Galapagos Islands, endogenous retroviruses, swine flu, avian flu, HIV-1, homologous structures, vestigial structures, population genetics, mutation, recombination, genetic drift. You can have 44 words back.

But that's like me giving an atheist "evidence" that the Bible is the Word of God by naming forty-four of the sixty-six books of the Bible and then saying, "Prove me wrong." His job would then be to work through each book trying to prove that it's not the Word of God.

So, let's start using that method. "Pakicetus" is believed to be a land animal about the size of a wolf and very similar in form to the related mesonychids, another extinct wolfish creature. Both of these creatures are said to be evidence of evolution. Yet, I believe that all it proves is that God created two more wolfish creatures along with the other 1.4 million difference species in creation.

But what you and I believe about anything is irrelevant when it comes to truth. If I lived in the time when science believed that the earth was flat and listed one hundred eminent scientists of my day to back up my beliefs, it wouldn't change the reality that the earth isn't flat. And no matter what we believe about our origins, creation tells us that there is an initial cause and that the Creator must have been somewhat more intelligent than man, as the most intelligent of us can't create a grain of rice from nothing, let alone birds, trees, flowers, the marvels of the human eye, etc.

Here are some more evolution believers' testimonies as to why they believe:

> The simple fact that it makes sense. It's only "too fantastic" if you've already decided in a creator, but if you come onto evolution clean, it's all very simple and logical. For every "problem" there's either a genuine answer, checked and rechecked by the entire scientific community, or an honest and sincere admission that we simply don't know. That's the thing, Ray, we allow ourselves to not know everything. We realize there's still mystery in the world. There's a reason that which we don't know is called "unknown."

> One hundred words are hardly sufficient and limiting the comments length on a subject like this is hardly reasonable since the response by nature of the question will be much longer. However, the reason that Evolution is a scientific fact is that it explains the phenomena within its scope and makes predictions and retro dictions regarding the natural world. From a simple observation of the similarities between species on our planet we can predict that there will be genetic similarities, which there are. We can also predict that we should find fossils indicating a progression of species within the fossil record, which we do. Furthermore, when coupled with the Germ Theory of disease we expect to see new strains of disease (virus and bacteria) Evolving with greater and greater potency, something we see with the recent swine flu, avian influenza and Disease Resistant Bacteria created by Immunizations and Antibiotic treatments.

The proof of a scientific theory is in its ability to correctly predict future discoveries which Evolution has done time and time again.

The fact that different species on this earth have similarities is not proof of evolution. It simply shows that God used the same blueprint for much of His creation: two eyes, two ears, a brain, blood, heart, kidneys, liver, lungs, male and female. These similarities can be found in elephants, horses, cows, primates, giraffes, donkeys, pigs, and over a million species. Neither is disease evidence for species-to-species Darwinian evolution. Its existence in all of creation is a testimony to the biblical truth that we live in a disease-ridden "fallen" creation.

I know evolution is scientific fact because it is truly astounding to me that the scientists that gave us flight, medicine, computers, astronomy, physics, chemistry, and the rest; all lost their minds and created fantasy when they turned to study the origin of the current life forms on this planet. Marsupials in Antarctica, there is a good one to explain…

In other words, scientists could never be wrong. Yet the ever-changing, ever-learning nature of science (the fact that they are continually wrong and change their beliefs) is ignored by many atheists. What science is assured of as the truth today will be corrected tomorrow and seen as a joke in future centuries. This isn't conjecture on my part, but a historical fact. Science changes.

The vast sums of evidence that are *easily* found on the Internet, in museums, researched daily in labs, predicted by scientists, etc., etc. The fact is that you are pushing all of this evidence to the side because your doctrine tells you otherwise.

Nested hierarchies. No need for the other 98 words.

Because it's more logical to trust the hard evidence in the fossil record which shows progression of multiple species, than an inconsistent, faulty man-made book, which has shown to be historically and archaeologically incorrect.

The fossil record shows changes *within* species. It speaks of special creation. It doesn't show evidence of species-to-species change.

100 Words? Try One: "Evidence." All of it points straight to evolution, and directly away from special creation. Every new piece of evidence continues to build on evolution for decades now, and there has yet to come a good piece of evidence for creation since, well, ever.

I have asked many confident believers in evolution to pinpoint "evidence" for me, and they usually say "Science." Or they say, "Fossils." When asked what science and what fossils, they usually reply, "I'm not an expert."

Intelligence. You may keep the other 99.

Evolution still stands strong, and as such, is still a scientific fact.

A number of Christians weighed in on the argument:

The theory of evolution is a fact supported by evidence from fields of scientific study such as paleontology, comparative anatomy, molecular biology, comparative biochemistry and physiology and observed speciation. All of which independently support evolution and verify one another.

Evolution is a theory. A theory is nothing more than conjecture or speculation. It has never been proven otherwise atheists would be showing this evidence to everyone. Instead, they speak in generalizations. I have asked several actual scientists, who happen to be atheists, if they had proof of evolution. They ALL said that yes there is proof and evolution has been proven. I asked them to show me the proof, or describe the proof. And every time I get the answer of "the proof is too much for any one person to understand." So I then ask them, "how is it you understand this proof?" to which I get silence, or ad hominem attacks.

Yeah, Yeah. I know I am not a scientist, don't believe in science, believe in God and believe in the Bible. So I am therefore stupid as well.

And whoever believes that archeology has proven the Bible to be untrue is just down right deceived. Archeologists very often use the stories in the Bible to lead them to many archeological finds. But just for the Middle East.

Oh but that is just my opinion.

Answer this, atheists, You have stated that the Bible is proven false. Please provide proof of this to be true. And please, don't come back and say it is a negative, you cannot prove a negative. Yes you can.

You state that the Bible was written by goat herders two to four thousand years ago. Then why is its historical record so accurate? Why is it that it predicted that Israel would be a nation again, and lo and behold it is a nation again? Why is it they predicted the geopolitical predicament we are in? When they had no geopolitical history to examine? Why is it they knew Israel would be hated by the entire world? Why?

I was convinced that evolution was a scientific fact because I was taught in middle school and again in high school and more in college. I never really questioned the theory. I assumed my teachers were telling the truth. I basically put my faith in their wisdom.

I see a lot of those types of answers from the atheists on this post. They say the word "evidence" but never back it up.

They point to scientists but never can explain what the "facts" are. I'm glad that I opened my mind and started to question the theory. When I began to look for the actual "evidence" for evolution, I quickly learned that it's not there. It's a worldview philosophy and not science. I suppose if someone doesn't believe in God there isn't anything else to cling to accept evolution.

When Creationists say they don't believe in evolution, they are not talking about microevolution. They are referring to macroevolution. Microevolution is a credibly observed scientific phenomena. What Creationists do not believe in is Darwin's macroevolutionary extrapolation of microevolution. Unlike microevolution, there is no truly scientific evidence for macroevolution, and in fact, there is significant evidence against it. The distinction between microevolution and macroevolution is, therefore, an important one for those interested in the creation vs. evolution debate.

"The library in the Louvre in Paris has three and a half miles of books on science. Most every one of them is obsolete. Smart scientists in lab coats wrote many of them."

Smart scientists in lab coats is not proof. The accepted science of yesterday is not necessarily the science of today. The library in the Louvre in Paris has three and a half miles of books on science. Most every one of them is obsolete. Smart scientists in lab coats wrote many of them. Yet today they are obsolete. Interesting. In 1861, the French Academy of Science wrote a pamphlet stating there were fifty-one incontrovertible scientific facts that proved the Bible not true.

Today there is not a reputable scientist on Earth that believes one of those fifty-one so-called facts (words from Pastor Adrian Rogers).

The point is, science can be good. Science can work. But science is often wrong. And many times when one waits a certain number of years "scientific laws" are found to be nothing. Interesting that evolution is not even a law (and don't use the gravity "theory," we have all heard it and it's ridiculous).

The Bible is the only book I have ever read that has given me the answers to life. I've never found answers to most of my questions in any other book.

PS: There are hundreds, even thousands, of scientists with excellent education who do not agree with evolution. There are thousands of scientists, from all types of scientific backgrounds, who are Christians. Just some food for thought. If nothing else it may make you think.

Personally I used to believe in evolution and say that God is real and that he created evolution during the time that the earth rotated slowly around when it first formed which would make days longer. I did all of this to make them both make sense (evolution and creation). In the end, I began to realize that macroevolution is practically impossible for the fact that it is impractical to believe that genetic mutations can create different numbers of chromosomes in species, that started out as a cell, that are able to reproduce. Down syndrome people are sterile, for example. Also if for some reason they could reproduce they would need a creature that had the same number of chromosomes to somehow be there at the same time, which if its evolution is unlikely. Now you have to decide at what point did a heart come in? Was it just a random piece of meat that later on developed a purpose? It had to be in order for that to be true considering that many prehistoric creatures had open blood circulation systems. That is why I don't believe in evolution anymore.

CHARLES DARWIN BELIEVED MAN EVOLVED FROM MONKEYS

"Ray, you have been told, over and over again, that no one believes humans came from monkeys. No one. Humans and monkeys share a common ancestor, which is stunningly obvious to anyone who has ever seen both a human and a monkey. Stop it."

"Whether the bishop likes it or not, Turkana Boy is a distant relation of his. *The bishop is descended from the apes* and these fossils tell how he evolved." Richard Leakey, paleoanthropologist (italics added).

"We admit that we are like apes, but we seldom realize that we are apes." Richard Dawkins

Primates are members of the taxonomic order Primate, a subgroup of mammals (class Mammalia). There are approximately 350 species of primate.

"What are the four categories of primates? 1. Prosimians, 2. New World Monkeys, 3. Old World Monkeys, 4. Apes."[5]

"Still we are monkeys, the sort of monkey which is called an ape. The common ancestor of apes and humans (humans are also perhaps best called apes I'd say) would have come in the group we call monkeys, and indeed old world monkeys. So we can say we are monkeys just as we are primates and mammals. If you look at the classification in the Wikipedia article on monkeys you will see that humans are actually classed there as apes, who are old world monkeys" (evolution believer).

Where would he get such a thought? From Charles Darwin (1871):

> But a naturalist would undoubtedly have ranked as an ape or a monkey, an ancient form which possesses many characters common to the Catarhine and Platyrhine monkeys, other characters in an intermediate condition, and some few, perhaps, distinct from those now found in either group. And as man from a genealogical point of view belongs to the Catarhine or Old World stock, we must conclude, however much the conclusion may revolt our pride, that our early progenitors would have been properly designated. But we must not fall into the error of supposing that the early progenitors of the whole Simian stock, including man, was identical with, or even closely resembled, any existing ape or monkey.

Interpretation: "Even though it's a revolting thought, our early ancestors were monkeys. But don't fall into the error of thinking that they looked like contemporary apes or monkeys."

THE CATHOLIC CHURCH AND EVOLUTION

The Catholic Church released a statement recently saying that Christianity is compatible with evolution. I released one saying that the two are not at all compatible. Genesis says that God made man in His own image (a moral entity), as male and female, with the ability to reproduce after their own kind (within their own species). Jesus affirmed this by saying "In the beginning God made them male and female" (Mark 10:6). The Scriptures also differentiate between the flesh of animals and the flesh of human beings—"All flesh is not the same flesh: but there is one kind of flesh of men, another flesh of beasts, another of fishes, and another of birds" (1 Corinthians 15:39). The closest they can get for human skin grafts is pig skin, and even then the graft may not take.

William Donahue, the eloquent and intelligent president of the Catholic League, responded with the heading "The simple mind of Ray Comfort," and rightly called me a "Protestant." He said, "Protestant author Ray Comfort recently said that 'the Vatican has chosen to officially believe Darwin rather than Jesus.' He accuses the Catholic Church of failing to exercise 'common sense' and of failing to think 'too deeply' about evolution."

The Vatican, in essence, is saying "Don't believe Jesus or Genesis. Believe Darwin instead." He even goes so far as to say that "In the name of diversity, the Vatican is encouraging atheism, and that's a terrible betrayal of Christianity."

SMILE TEST

A little girl asked her mother, "How did the human race appear?" The mother answered, "God made Adam and Eve; they had children; and so was all mankind made." Two days later the girl asked her father the same question. The father answered, "Many years ago there were monkeys from which the human race evolved." The confused girl returned to her mother and said, "Mom, how is it possible that you told me the human race was created by God, and Dad said they developed from monkeys?" The mother answered, "Well, Dear, it is very simple. I told you about my side of the family, and your father told you about his!"

CHAPTER THIRTEEN

THE ATHEIST'S AMAZING IMAGINATION

H ISTORY HAS shown that man has often used the name of God for his own agenda—from religious wars, to Adolf Hitler (who had "God with us" engraved on the belt buckles of Nazi Germany). The zealous evolutionist evokes the name of science in the same way, and as far as he is concerned, anyone who disagrees with his beliefs disagrees with science and is therefore ignorant.

Evolutionary "scientists" would excel as Disney imagineers. Take for example the gifted folks at the very popular The Future is Wild ministry. These secular prophets predict the future. They give long-term evolutionary horoscopes for the earth—what evolution may do in 100 million years time, all in the name of science.

They do with the future what believers in evolution do with the past. They imagine. Then they draw pictures of what they believe may happen and sell them to kids and those with the imagination of a child. They say, "Every animal and plant in *The Future is Wild* could really exist. Our science team devised each one as a viable, living organism.... It's not surprising that our scientists talk about them as if they really existed!"

The same goes for those who imagine what things were like up to 14 billion years into the past, and talk about them as if they weren't really imagining. All in the name of science. Imagine that.

The Open Mind of an Atheist

In reference to the biblical story of Adam and Eve, an atheist cynically said:

> "Well, I suppose that if you can believe in talking snakes you can believe anything." But did you know that a gorilla can learn thousands of English words and has the capacity to use language?
>
> "More recently, the striking achievements of Kanzi, a bonobo who apparently has learned more than 3,000 spoken English words and can produce (by means of lexigrams) novel English sentences and comprehend English sentences he has never heard before, has strengthened the case of those who argue that the thinking of higher apes is much more complex than had previously been assumed and that the capacity for language use, at least at a rudimentary level, is not exclusively human."

Do you believe in talking birds? Do you think porpoises speak to each other? How about whales? Do dogs communicate to each other? Do you think they understand English words? Have you ever spoken to a dog? Has a dog or cat ever "told" you that it was hungry? Have you ever heard of dogs warning their owners of a fire in their home? I presume that you believe that man evolved from fish. Why then is your mind so closed to the possibility that an animal could communicate with humans? It seems that the atheist mind is open to anything as long as it's not in the Bible. I wonder why?

Do you think fire existed before man discovered it? Of course it did. Even though no one had ever seen it, but it was a hidden reality (within the laws of nature).

It is interesting to note that fire manifests itself only when it has something to consume. If there is nothing material or no oxygen left for it to burn, its rage dissipates, and it disappears from our sight.

The Bible continually likens the justice of God to a "consuming fire." It is passive until there is injustice. However, don't make the tragic mistake of thinking that it doesn't exist just because you can't see it. And don't be deceived into thinking that the patience of God is a sign that He has no knowledge of your sins. The day will come when the Law of God will manifest in rage upon everything that is evil. The justice of God will come "In flaming fire taking vengeance on them that know not God, and that obey not the gospel of our Lord Jesus Christ…" (2 Thessalonians 1:8).

You may be familiar with Moses and the burning bush. It raged with fire, and yet the bush wasn't consumed: "And the angel of the Lord appeared to him in a flame of fire out of the midst of a bush: and he looked, and, behold, the bush burned with fire, and the bush was not consumed" (Exodus 3:2). As Moses approached the bush, God told him to take off his shoes (a gesture of humility) because the land on which he stood was holy ground. As Moses did so, he was allowed to approach God and he wasn't consumed for his sins.

God (in His kindness) has made a way where we may approach Him and not be consumed by the wrath of His Law. He did it by becoming a human being and receiving the fire of His wrath upon Himself, so that it wouldn't have to fall on guilty sinners. He paid the fine so that we could leave the courtroom. God can legally dismiss our case. So humble yourself today and approach God through the blood of the Cross, and He will dismiss your case and allow you to live: "Wherefore we receiving a kingdom which cannot be moved, let us have grace, whereby we may serve God acceptably with reverence and godly fear: for our God is a consuming fire" (Hebrews 12:28-29).

According to the News Bureau at the University of Illinois:

> Life did not begin with one primordial cell. Instead, there were initially at least three simple types of loosely constructed cellular organizations. They swam in a pool of genes, evolving in a communal way that aided one another in bootstrapping into the three distinct types of cells by sharing their evolutionary inventions.

I have some news for the University News Bureau. If you talk about life beginning as a "loosely constructed cellular organizations" that swam "in a pool of genes," then it wasn't the beginning at all, because loosely constructed cellular organizations swimming in a pool of genes *already existed.*

Ex-atheist Lee Strobel said, "Essentially, I realized that to stay an atheist, I would have to believe that nothing produces everything; non-life produces life; randomness produces fine-tuning; chaos produces information; unconsciousness produces consciousness; and non-reason produces reason. Those leaps of faith were simply too big for me to take…"

For the beginning to be the beginning, there must be nothing. Zilch. If you disagree, in simple language, explain to me where I am going wrong. Tell me what was in the beginning— what was it that began the evolutionary process? Let me guess your answer. You don't know what it was, but you know that it wasn't God.

GETTING THINGS HUMMING

A group of leading evolutionary biologists have gathered together in an effort to create a living hummingbird. Rather than "cheating" by using existing material, they have decided to duplicate the actual beginning of creation. They have determined to begin the process from nothing, as in the genesis of life's origins.

They have already begun by listing what they need to create the small but intricate male bird. They require some sort of bone material to make lightweight hollow bones, very strong heart muscle, living blood, a variety of feather material, substance to make a long beak and even longer tongue, two eyes, a digestive system, lungs, kidneys, a liver, an appetite, an instinct to survive, a fear of predators, the ability to find and recognize a mate, and the ability to reproduce after its own kind. They will also need to make the ability to instinctively create a nest and raise young, and of course the ability to fly forward, backward, and sideway, and to remain stationary in the air.

Unfortunately, they are not sure how to create what they need, using nothing, as in the beginning. They have admitted that that's their only problem. They are restricted to using nothing to create something, as in the beginning. They don't know what to do next and they don't know who to ask. Still, they are adamant that as soon as they discover how to make something from nothing, the process will begin. It's simply a lack of time and of understanding.

Meanwhile, the men have formed a commission to discuss their problem, and named it the "Don't Understand How" committee. "DUH" for short.

> For the invisible things of him from the creation of the world are clearly seen, being understood by the things that are made, even his eternal power and Godhead; so that they

are without excuse: because that, when they knew God, they glorified him not as God, neither were thankful; but became vain in their imaginations, and their foolish heart was darkened (Romans 1:20-21).

TOUGH ANSWERS FOR ATHEISTS

I watched a short video (presumably presented by an atheist) called "Tough Question for Christians" recently. He began his tough question by saying that he had videotape evidence that you dented his car. He gave you twenty-four hours to apologize, and if you didn't, he was going to throw gasoline on you and burn you alive. That *is* tough.

He then compared his analogy with the message of Christianity, saying that sinning against God was like denting a car, and that God will burn people in Hell for "not believing in Him" and for any other "little, tiny thing" they may have done.

Let's look at a more applicable analogy. The police discover the grisly scene of six mutilated bodies of teenage girls who were tied up, tortured, viciously raped, and then had their throats cut. They have your fingerprints on the knife, your DNA at the crime scene, and videotape of you boasting to a friend about how terrified the girls were when you slowly cut their throats. You thought that was funny.

The judge finds you guilty of the heinous crimes of rape and murder of the six girls, and sentences you to death by the electric chair. You react by saying, "My crime was petty. It was no big deal. This judge is evil."

The atheist's mistake is to think that the God he doesn't believe in has the same moral standards as humanity. Yet the God he must face on Judgment Day is morally perfect and utterly holy. He considers lust to be adultery and hatred to be murder. We are told in Scripture that lying lips are an abomination to

Him. He killed a husband and wife (in the Book of Acts) simply because they told one lie. Lying is so serious to Him the Bible warns that all liars will have their part in the lake of fire. Sin is not about "little, tiny things" that we have done. It is deadly serious.

Yet God is rich in mercy toward us. Isn't that true? More than likely you have lied, looked with lust, stolen, blasphemed His name, etc., and yet He hasn't treated you according to your sins and struck you dead. Well, not yet. But it will happen one day, and then you have to face Him for all those unspeakably serious crimes against His Law.

The other mistake the atheist made was to think that people will end up in Hell for not believing in God. That's just not true. Plenty of people who believe in God will end up in Hell. Among them will be the many religious hypocrites and millions of others who were warned of the reality of Hell but refused to repent and trust the Savior.

> *Plenty of people who believe in God will end up in Hell. Among them will be the many religious hypocrites and millions who were warned of the reality of Hell but refused to repent and trust the Savior.*

God has no pleasure in your death. If you find yourself in Hell, you will have no one to blame but yourself. The Bible warns that our damnation is just. Justice will certainly be done if His mercy is spurned.

Theist Christopher Geiser said: "Math teachers are not seen as narrowminded when they say there is only one answer to 2+2." Antagonist Jason replied, "They can also demonstrate that answer."

But math teachers cannot demonstrate anything to someone who is unreasonable. If an unreasonable person (for some reason) wanted to change the definition of the number 2, and then say that the second 2 was not the same quantity as the first, you have a stalemate. To argue any logic, you need both parties to be reasonable.

This is the problem theists have with those who believe themselves to be atheists. The fact that there cannot be a creation without a creator is reasonable common sense. That common sense is abandoned by the atheist. He keeps coming back and parroting "Show me the evidence," when the evidence is as plain as 2+2=4.

Aristotle once stated: "It is impossible that movement should ever come into being or cease to be, for it must always have existed. Nor can time come into being or cease to be." Scientists now know better. They say, "Current theories hold that about 5 billion years ago the sun began to form from a huge dark cloud of dust and vapor that included the remnants of earlier stars which had exploded." Other experts tell us that "the Sun was also born in such a cluster, around 4.6 billion years ago, along with thousands of young stars."

So it is well accepted in the scientific community that the sun had a beginning. Here's my question: Where did the huge dark cloud of dust and vapor that included the remnants of earlier stars come from? It, too, must have had a beginning. Who or what created it, shaped it into the sun, and placed it at just the right distance from the earth so that life could begin? To say that the dust and vapor were eternal is to go back to Aristotle's erroneous belief, which violates the second law of thermodynamics. What is the scientific explanation for where the dust and vapor came from? Atheists don't have one. Theists do.

HOW BIG IS THE UNIVERSE?

"I would like to hear your quantitative answers as to how big the universe is, what light is, and what life is. Since

God has revealed all of these answers to you in the Bible, I'm sure that these answers will be answered with 100% precision, and will be reflected in current observations."

I have no faith in "current" observations. Every generation thinks that they are current—that they are "modern." In twenty years' time they will laugh at current clothes and hair styles. In a hundred years what science believes today will be a joke, and they will no doubt believe that their current knowledge is cool. Man's quantitative knowledge is a tiny drop in the ocean of what actually is absolute truth.

To use the word "big" in describing the universe shows the smallness of our minds. If an elephant is *big*, what word describes the universe? The best one I can currently come up with is the "infinitude" of the universe. There's not a wall around the edge of space. Traveling at the speed of light, you would go on forever, no matter in which direction you travel. But one thing I do know: God fills the universe. That's a big brain-strain.

He is also the source of light and the source of life. Around 800 years before Christ, the Psalmist maintained this: "For with you is the fountain of life: in your light shall we see light" (Psalm 36:9). In speaking of the Messiah, John said the same thing: "In him was life; and the life was the light of men" (John 1:4). Jesus said the same thing of Himself: "Then spoke Jesus again to them, saying, I am the light of the world: he that follows me shall not walk in darkness, but shall have the light of life" (John 8:12).

Then the Apostle Paul confirms this with his: "But is now made manifest by the appearing of our Savior Jesus Christ, who has abolished death, and has brought life and immortality to light through the gospel" (2 Timothy 1:10). There you are. That's 100 percent precision, straight from the ever-current Bible.

Ask most atheists what was in the beginning and they will say "Evolution." Press them on what was before evolution—what was its initial cause, and they will be stumped. They cannot give an answer as to where the material came from for evolution to bring life into being. For the initial cause to make sense, it had to be something that was immaterial (nonmaterial), which God is. The Bible says that it was the *Spirit* of God that moved upon the face of the waters (see Genesis 1:2).

So that brings the atheist to his only defense. He asks, "Who then made God?" His real dilemma isn't that he believes that God doesn't exist, but that he doesn't understand how God could exist eternally. If that's the case, then every human being is an atheist. No one can wrap his finite mind around the eternal nature of God.

> *The atheist's real dilemma isn't that he believes that God doesn't exist, but that he doesn't understand how God could exist eternally. If that's the case, then every human being is an atheist.*

However, who among us can comprehend the infinitude of space? Imagine sending an incredibly powerful laser beam into space and it traveling in a particular direction for tens of billions of trillions of miles. It will never reach an end. Now move your beam slightly to the right of that first direction in which you pointed it, and send it tens of billions of trillions of miles, and it will never come to the end of space. Repeat the beam exercise a million times in a million different directions, and never will you come to an end of an infinite space in any direction you point it.

Such thoughts become too much for the human mind, and thoughts of God and His eternal nature are the same. But there is something that can make the mind ache even more. Go back to the thoughts of the immensity of space. Get a grip on all those different beams of light going for hundreds of billions of trillions of miles in tens of millions of directions, each beam moving an infinite distance away from the other beams, as it reaches into space.

Think how "large" space is, then say to yourself that God made it. But more than that, He fills space with His presence. He is omnipresent (everywhere at once). But even more than that, He is as much "God" at a point a billion trillion miles into space as He is in your presence at this moment of time. He is not divided in thought.

Then add to that the fact that He holds all knowledge of every thought and deed of every human being in His infinite mind, and you have scratched the tiny surface of the surface of thought about the greatness of God.

CHAPTER FOURTEEN

THE POWER OF THE IMAGINATION

A THEISTS FLATLY reject the Genesis Fall, in which we are given the biblical explanation as to why there is disease, suffering, and death. So they have no account for the suffering of this world. It is because of this, that they will often quote Monty Python: "All things sick and cancerous, all evil great and small, Putrid foul and gangrenous, the Lord God made them all…" Their thought is that if God did exist, then He alone, not man, is responsible for the pains of this world.

The normal "idolater" creates a version of God to which he can snuggle up. He quote-mines Scripture and creates an all-loving, kind, and forgiving God. He leaves out the fact that the Bible tells us that God is holy and just, and will by no means clear the guilty. He passes over verses such as "Everyone proud in heart is an abomination to the Lord; though they join forces, none will go unpunished" (Proverbs 16:5). Then once he has created his benevolent image of God, he bows before it, and it is to that image that he brings his prayerful petitions. The problem is, his god doesn't exist. But that is of no consequence to him, because the idolater can easily find a church that preaches the attributes of his idol. Under the sound of the many modern pulpits, his faith will grow as he listens to sermons that confirm his error.

The atheist does the opposite of the regular idolater. He quote-mines the Scriptures and searches out the harsher judgments of God and builds an image of God he finds to be repulsive. Then, once he has made his idol, he flatly rejects it. *And so he should.* The image that he has made of God is evil. It is without love and mercy. And so the atheist has the same problem as the idolater. The image only exists in the atheist's place of imagery... in his imagination.

BY THE LIGHT OF THE SILVERY MOON

"If you have proof the Bible is wrong I would hope you are a kind enough person to share it with all us misguided children of the Light...I am hoping you agree with just about everyone in knowing that the moon is not a source of light. In which case: Genesis 1:16 is wrong ['And God made two great lights; the greater light to rule the day, and the lesser light to rule the night: he made the stars also']."

You had better contact those misguided folks who compile dictionaries. Have them remove the word "moonlight." They say: moonlight—noun, "the light of the moon." Also have Shakespeare's "Midsummer Night's Dream" banned from learning institutions. William wrote: "Thou hast by moonlight at her window sung..."

Then contact the ignorant scientists at NASA. They are deceived into thinking that moonlight exists: "Moonlight, remember, is no more exotic than sunlight reflected from the dusty surface of the moon. The only difference is intensity: Moonlight is about 400,000 times fainter than direct sunlight." Don't leave out country singer and writer LeAnn Rimes for her mistaken hit "Can't

Fight the Moonlight," and the producers of the hit TV series "Moonlight."

All these mentally challenged folks are uneducated flat-earthers who need to sit at the feet of the intelligent modern atheist and learn that there's no such thing as moonlight.

If a man throws a shoe at a dog, nothing much happens. However, if he throws a shoe at a head of state and calls him a "dog," something big happens. The perpetrator is arrested and may face up to seventeen years in prison. His crime escalates according to whom it is committed against. This may be a strange thing to have to explain, but the man goes to jail *even if he doesn't believe that jail exists.*

When we sin we violate the Moral Law and sin directly against God (see Psalm 51:4). The Law has already arrested us (see 2 Peter 3:7). We are not going to escape (Romans 2:3). If we die in our sins, the divine Law will eventually execute us and send us to Hell (Revelation 21:8). This will happen even if we do not believe in the existence of Hell.

The problem with the atheist is that he doesn't believe in his own quote-mined version of God. He has an image of God that doesn't exist. He is only an atheist in his own mind.

He needs to pull back the curtains and think of the infinitude of space and the immensity of creation. Then think of the immensity of the God who created all these things. When those thoughts are allowed to flood his brain, he should then add the thought that this Creator is perfect and holy, and is to be feared.

It is that healthy fear of God (the beginning of wisdom) that will send us to the Cross. There we may taste the sweetness of mercy rather than the bitterness of His terrible wrath: "He is trampling out the vintage where the grapes of wrath are stored. He hath loosed the fateful lightning of His terrible swift sword; Oh, be swift, my soul, to answer Him! be jubilant, my feet!"

AN IMPORTANT QUESTION

An atheist argued, "Jesus didn't abolish death. People still die and, as before His birth, peoples' souls still live on forever."

Of course people still die. However, the Bible still says, "Jesus Christ abolished death" (2 Timothy 1:10). So you have a choice. Either those who believe that death has been abolished are mentally challenged, or there is something here that you don't yet understand.

The Scriptures tell us that sin has resulted in capital punishment for humanity (see Romans 6:23). We die because we are criminals in God's sight. However, for those who repent and trust in the Savior, that death sentence is instantly commuted. It is nullified. God shows us the immutability of His promise of commutation by giving us His Holy Spirit. The Bible says that He "seals" us with His Spirit as a token of good faith, so that we have even more than His promise.

It's as though God said that He abolished darkness and then quietly gave a secret light to those that trust Him (see Psalm 25:14). So each person who has the light no longer walks in darkness—they have "the light of life." This is what Jesus was speaking of when He said, "I am the light of the world: he that follows me shall not walk in darkness, but shall have the light of life" (John 8:12).

BERKELEY BRAINWASHING—TREES ARE OUR COUSINS

Biological evolution, simply put, is descent with modification. This definition encompasses small-scale evolution (changes in gene frequency in a population from one generation to the next) and large-scale evolution (the descent of different species from a common ancestor over many generations). Evolution helps us to understand the history of life. Biological evolution is not simply a matter of change over time. Lots of things change over time: trees lose their leaves, mountain ranges rise and erode, but they aren't examples of biological evolution because they don't involve descent through genetic inheritance. The central idea of biological evolution is that all life on Earth shares a common ancestor, just as you and your cousins share a common grandmother. Through the process of descent with modification, the common ancestor of life on Earth gave rise to the fantastic diversity that we see documented in the fossil record and around us today. Evolution means that we're all distant cousins: humans and oak trees, hummingbirds and whales.[1]

I was listening to the "Hallelujah Chorus" of Handel's *Messiah* recently and wondering what atheists have as an equivalent. An equivalent? They don't have a Bible, they don't belong to a church, they don't have a relationship with God, and they don't have their own music. That's because they have nothing to sing about. Without God, atheism would have no reason to exist.

The Scriptures tell us that sin has resulted in capital punishment for humanity. However, for those who repent and trust in the Savior, that death sentence is instantly commuted.

God bless Handel for using his God-given gifts to glorify the Giver. God gave man the ability to create music, and godly music has the ability to give us a small taste of Heaven.

What an incredible heritage we have as Christians. How rich biblical Christianity is in history. Its missionaries have taken the message of salvation to the ends of the earth.

And what a glorious future it promises: "Jesus Christ has abolished death and brought life and immortality to light through the gospel."

WHEN TRAGEDY STRIKES

My eyes have been leaking a lot lately. Back in 2008, I found it hard to clearly focus on a news item that showed a San Diego man at a press conference, reacting to the tragic deaths of his wife, his two young daughters, and his mother-in-law. A fighter jet had landed on his house, and, in an instant, swept them into eternity.

As he leaned for support on his pastor's arms, he said that he didn't have any animosity towards the pilot of the downed plane, calling him a "hero." Then he said, "I know there are many people who have experienced more terrible things. Please tell me how to do it, because I don't know what to do."

It seems that everything this man leaned on for security—his beloved family and even his home, were taken from him. He told reporters: "Nobody expected such a horrible thing to happen, especially right here, right [in] our house. I know God is taking care of my [family]."

In times of such despair, there is great consolation in Christianity. God promises to work this tragic incident out for his good: "And we know that all things work together for good to them that love God, to them who are the called according to his purpose" (Romans 8:28).

THE ANVIL OF ETERNAL JUSTICE

In a recent political scandal, commentators spoke of a "culture of corruption" surrounding a certain high-profile politician. In reference to the fact that he had violated the law, one commentator said, "The line kept moving," and that he seemed to have "lost his moral compass."

That's the result of the theory of relativity. Mankind has a theory that there is no absolute right and absolute wrong. The strange thing about it is, he is absolutely sure that he's right when he says that no one can be absolutely sure about anything. The political commentators also said that he thought he was invulnerable. Pride and arrogance are often the bedfellows of corruption.

The fallen political figure is typical of the proud human heart. He lives in a culture of corruption where he pushes the moral envelope. Like the proud politician, he thinks he's invulnerable. However, the line of right and wrong is not relative. It is written in stone. It doesn't change, move, or soften. When the Moral Law is violated, the sinner becomes an anvil for eternal justice. Time will show that to be true.

The political commentators called the politician "ethically challenged." That's modern vernacular for saying that they thought he was a criminal. The only way to prove that is to try him by civil law.

The same applies to you and me. We are extremely ethically challenged. If found guilty on Judgment Day we will go away for more than a long time. It will be for eternity. But the Judge is rich in mercy, and He kindly offers us a reprieve in the Gospel. Read about it in the New Testament. Do it today. You may not have tomorrow.

THE INVESTIGATOR

An investigator was asked to listen to the testimony of four eye witnesses to a bank robbery. He found that three of the witnesses said that there were only two bank robbers, while the fourth disagreed. He adamantly maintained that there were three.

Did the investigator therefore conclude that the bank robbery didn't take place? Of course not. He began to think deeply as to how the testimonies could harmonize, and rightly came to the conclusion that one of the bank employees had been an accomplice to the robbery.

If, for some reason, the investigator had the preconceived notion that all the witnesses were liars, he wouldn't be an "investigator." If he is seeking the truth, he must set aside all personal prejudice and attempt (within the bounds of reason) to harmonize his eyewitness testimonies.

If anyone wants to investigate the "contradictions" of the testimony of the gospels, he must put aside preconceived notions—all personal prejudice, and humbly seek the truth. For those who do so, it doesn't take long to see their perfect harmony.

I thank God for fear. It keeps me from harm. Fear stops me going near the edge of a thousand-foot cliff. It keeps me away from poisonous spiders and snakes. It tells me to put on a seat belt. Fear stops me from taking risks when I'm on the top of a ladder and can't reach something.

Fear has a bedfellow—it is called "common sense." Common sense stops me from going near the edge of a thousand-foot cliff, keeps me from poisonous spiders and snakes. Common sense tells me to put on a seat belt. The two, fear and common sense, go hand in hand. That sort of fear is good.

There is also a fear that is bad. The Bible says that it has "torment." That's not the fear to which I am referring.

Contrary to what many may think, I am not a "Hell-fire preacher." I believe that Hell is a real place and I therefore continually warn of its reality, but I don't think that people should become Christians because of a fear of Hell. Rather, they should come to Christ out of a fear of the God that can cast them into Hell:

And I say to you, My friends, do not be afraid of those who kill the body, and after that have no more that they can do. But I will show you whom you should fear: Fear Him who, after He has killed, has power to cast into hell; yes, I say to you, fear Him!" (Luke 12:4-5).

So what's the difference between fearing Hell and fearing God? The two are separated by the Moral Law. It is the Law (the Ten Commandments) that shows me that God is perfect and holy. The Law also shows me that I am not. It reveals that lust is adultery in the sight of God and that hatred is murder. It brings a knowledge of my depravity.

The Law shows me that I justly deserve Hell. It convinces me that I will be without excuse on the Day of Judgment. That's why the Bible warns that it is "a fearful thing to fall into the hands of the Living God." Those who fall into His holy hands will only be those who deliberately stepped off of the high cliffs of sin.

It's only when I realize that I deserve Hell that I can truly appreciate the love and mercy of God in providing a Savior.

It's only when I realize that I deserve Hell that I can truly appreciate the love and mercy of God in providing a Savior. Through trust in Jesus I still fear God, but I no longer fear Judgment Day because my sins have been forgiven. This is the meaning of "Herein is our love made perfect, that we may have boldness in the day of judgment: because as he is, so are we in this world" (1 John 4:17).

In December of 2008, a report which studied thirty thousand high school students found that 30 percent of students admitted to stealing from a store within the past year, a 2 percent rise from 2006. More than one-third of boys (35 percent) said they had stolen goods, compared to 26 percent of girls. An overwhelming majority, 83 percent of public school and private religious school students, admitted to lying to their parents about something significant, compared to 78 percent for those attending independent non-religious schools. "Despite these high levels of dishonesty, these same kids have a high self-image when it comes to ethics," the study reported. Some 93 percent of students indicated satisfaction with their own character and ethics, with 77 percent saying that "when it comes to doing what is right, I am better than most people I know."

These are violations of God's Law—lying, stealing, and dishonoring of parents. It's significant that the religious schools had higher rates of lawlessness and that self-righteousness was rampant. While experts and philosophers suggest a multitude of reasons as to why this is happening, it traces itself back to a lack of the fear of God. Their concept of God doesn't include retribution for transgression of His Law. Idolatry is probably the hardest to detect, but it is undoubtedly the worst of sins, because of the door it opens.

PAINTED INTO A CORNER

"Ray. I have no idea about what Darwin believed about the evolution of sex. I do not care. It is not a matter of name calling either. The problem is that you just assumed that Darwin postulated something because it was something about evolution. No lifetime has been so long that a single scientist could have solved all the questions about the theory by her/himself. This is the point (in case you missed it). What you really would have to know is not what Darwin thought about the evolution of sex, but what is currently known. In science we have no prophets, no messiahs. We work and work and work, and results get published, and knowledge increases. Why would I be limited to find out what, and 'if,' Darwin thought when there is a bunch of current knowledge that would give me a better perspective?"

It's not a matter of solving *all* the questions of his theory. It's only one of a million cans of worms he opened. When you eliminate a creator, you are stuck with the ramifications. We have male and female throughout creation. Darwin and every believer in evolution believes that male and female evolved. There was a time when there was no male and no female, and then over millions of years, they came about through the process of evolution to a point of having the ability to reproduce. You don't know how they reproduced before that point, but you are stuck with the fact that before there were both sexes the only way they could carry on their species, was to be asexual. That's unless you say that "in the beginning there was male and female," and that cuts too close to the Genesis bone for an atheist.

Charles Robert Darwin went to meet his maker on April 19, 1882, in Downe, England. Upon his death, Darwin's family arranged for him to be buried in St. Mary's churchyard in the village of Downe. However, William Spottiswoode, the president of the Royal Society, wrote to the dean of Westminster Abbey requesting that Darwin be buried in its prestigious cemetery. Darwin once wrote: "I feel most deeply that the whole subject is too profound for human intellect. A dog might as well speculate on the mind of Newton."

It's interesting that Darwin spoke of the mind of Newton. Here is what Newton said about God:

Repentance and the remission of sins relate to transgressions against the two first Commandments. We are to forsake the Devil, that is, all false gods and all manner of idolatry, this being a breach of the first and great commandment. And we are to forsake the flesh and the world, or as the Apostle John expressed it, the lust of the flesh and the lust of the eye and the pride of life, that is, unchastity, covetousness, pride and ambition; these things being a breach of the second of the two great Commandments.

And we are to believe in one God, the father, almighty in dominion, the Maker of heaven and earth and of all things therein, and in our Lord Jesus Christ, the son of God, who was born of a Virgin and sacrificed for us on the cross, and the third day rose again from the dead and ascended unto heaven…And as for the Christian worship, we are authorized in scripture to give glory and honor to God the Father, because he hath created all things, and to the Lamb of God, because he hath redeemed us with his blood and is our Lord, and to direct our prayers to God the Father in the name of Christ…"

Ironically, Charles Darwin is buried in Westminster Abbey, close to Sir Isaac Newton.

WHY DO FEMALES EXIST?

All animals, all fish and reptiles, have the ability to reproduce of their own kind because they have females within the species. No male can reproduce and keep its kind alive without a female of the same species. Dogs, cats, horses, cows, elephants, humans, giraffes, lions, tigers, birds, fish, and reptiles all came into being having both male and female. If any species came into existence without a mature female present (with complimentary female components), that one male would have remained alone and in time died. The species could not have survived without a female.

Why did hundreds of thousands of animals, fish, reptiles, and birds (over millions of years) evolve a female partner (that coincidentally matured at just the right time) with each species?

The evolutionary explanation of where male and female must have come from has angered some believers in the theory. It would strengthen the evolution case (instead of resorting to name-calling) to instead explain what Darwin did believe about the origin of male and female.

One Darwinian believer said:

> In fact, distinct gender emerged as a result of organisms being able to reproduce through the sharing of genetic information in reproduction. Initial "sexual" reproduction of this nature was essentially gender-neutral, as there was no "male" or "female" assignment because any given organism could share or receive compatible genetic information from another organism of the same species. Gender differentiation emerged as a result of specialization of this ability.

The contention between Darwin's theory of evolution and the Bible's account of creation is extremely significant. This is because if evolution is true, the Bible is a fallacy.

Darwin theorized that mankind (both male and female) evolved in their pre-human state alongside each other over millions of years, both reproducing after their own kind before the ability to physically have sex evolved. They did this through "asexuality" ("without sexual desire or activity or lacking any apparent sex or sex organs"). Each of them split in half: "Asexual organisms reproduce by fission (splitting in half)."[2]

> "Sexual reproduction would never have begun to evolve, and would never have continued to evolve to become as sophisticated as it is today in many plants and animals, unless it offered a significant evolutionary advantage. As to what this

advantage might be, however, is still the subject of continuing debate in the scientific community. Theories about the evolution of sex have proven to be very difficult to test experimentally, and so the answer is still very much open to speculation."[3]

In other words, they have no idea why pre-humans stopped splitting in half and started having sex, or why male and female exist throughout creation.

In contrast, the Bible maintains that God instantaneously created man (in His own image) and woman, giving them the ability to reproduce after their kind. So the Bible and the theory of Darwinian evolution are not only opposed to one another, they are incompatible. The only commonality is that they are both miraculous and they both require faith to believe them.

Those who believe in the theory of evolution are passionate, and for a good reason. If Darwin was right, man is simply an animal with no moral accountability, and his desires therefore to procreate are merely natural survival instincts.

However, if the Bible is true, it throws a huge, cold, and heavy wet blanket over man's desire to sow wild oats. It not only says that he is accountable, but that there will be severe retribution for his adultery, fornication, and even lust (see Matthew 5:27-28).

So if you are wavering between the two, you had better find out which one is true. There are no repercussions if evolution is true. However, if the Bible comes out the winner, you may find yourself losing your most precious possession (see Matthew 16:26).

AN ATHEIST'S HONEST QUESTION

"My question for you is, if the whole point of accepting Christ is that it makes you righteous, do you mean righteous as in compassionate, loving, etc...or righteous as in clean, pure, or saved? Or am I completely missing the point and you actually mean something else altogether? Because if it's the first one (compassionate, etc.), I think that many Christians and non-Christians alike fit that profile."

I will do my best to answer your question. There are two sorts of "righteousness" being spoken of here. Living a compassionate and clean life is a form of righteousness. It's living in a righteous way. However, the righteousness that we speak of in becoming a Christian is what is called "imputed" righteousness. This is the one that saves us from death and Hell. Let me try and explain with an analogy.

Let's say your father lost his wife years ago to a drunk driver and he strictly told you never to drink and drive. Even though you could drive a car, you didn't have a license, so you gave him your word that it would never happen.

But one night you had too much to drink and without his permission you grabbed your dad's keys and took your friends for a quick joyride in his new car.

You hit the freeway and decide to show them how quickly it accelerates. Suddenly a dog is in front of you! You swerve to miss the animal, and the next thing you know, you awake in the hospital with the police at your bedside. You not only destroyed your dad's new car, but you seriously injured your three friends, and ran two other vehicles off the road. You didn't have a license, and your blood alcohol level was off the charts. You are in big trouble.

At your trial, you can't begin to justify your actions. What could you say for your justification? What could get you off the hook? Could you say that you didn't mean to do what you did? That you were not drunk? That plenty of people drink and drive? That you are sorry and won't do it again? Of course you should be sorry, and of course you shouldn't do it again. You do the only thing you can do. You plead guilty.

The judge fines you $250,000 to cover damages, $100,000 for court costs, and $200,000 for the crimes of drunk driving and driving without a license. The total is $550,000 or imprisonment. You don't have two beans to rub together. You are horrified that you are going to prison for a long time.

Suddenly your dad steps up to the bailiff and asks to speak to the judge. He then gets out his checkbook, writes a check and gives it to the judge. The judge looks at the check, then at you, and says, "You father just paid your fine in full. You are free to go."

You find out later that your dad made a huge sacrifice to pay your fine. He sold his beloved house and used a lifetime of savings. He is now penniless; but his sacrifice has saved you from a long prison term. Tell me, how are you going to feel now about your dad and about his incredible sacrifice? You would be truly sorry for what you did, very humbled by what he did, and unspeakably grateful to him. Isn't that true?

You knew that you were a guilty criminal. The payment that your father handed the judge immediately made you right with the law.

In a sense, your father's sacrifice gave you a type of "imputed" righteousness. You couldn't justify yourself, let alone declare yourself righteous. You knew that you were a guilty criminal. It was your father's payment that "justified" you. The payment that he handed the judge immediately made you right with the law. It had no demands on you. You were declared righteous the moment it was paid. You did nothing to deserve it, and after a lifetime of living to please your dad, you still won't deserve it. It was his unmerited gift of love to you.

Here now is the message of Christianity. We have all deliberately violated God's Law. We willfully gave ourselves to the sins of lust, greed, lying, stealing, blasphemy, ingratitude, adultery, hatred, fornication, gossip, and anger. Keep in mind that God is so holy that He sees lust as adultery and hatred as murder, and that any sort of lying is so serious to Him that He warns that all liars will have their part in the lake of fire.

Who of us can justify ourselves under the light of that perfect Law (the Ten Commandments)? Dare we say that we are not guilty? Dare we say that our sins weren't willful, or that there are people worse than we are? Remember, the Moral Law shines into the heart. God sees your thought life. He sees the unclean sexual desires, the hidden sins of conceit, selfishness, envy, jealousy, etc.

If we stand before that Law on the Day of Judgment, it will justly condemn us to Hell. Our crimes against God have put us on death row. It patiently waits for the moment of our execution. We have nothing to offer the Judge in payment for our crimes. How could we ever make things right? We are without hope.

Hence, the Gospel. God sent His Son. He created a body for Himself, lived a perfect life, then paid the fine for the Law that we violated. He paid it through excruciating suffering. God commended His love toward us, in that, while we were yet sinners Christ died for us. Then He rose again on the third day. Now, upon our repentance and faith in Jesus, the Judge can legally dismiss our case. We couldn't justify ourselves, but God justified us (made us righteous) through the death of His Son.

It's important to understand that the Christian isn't simply a forgiven criminal. God actually clothes Him with the righteousness of Christ. This is "imputed" righteousness. It is difficult for us to conceive of such a thing, but that means (in God's eyes) the one who trusts in Jesus is made absolutely perfect, pure, holy, and righteous. This is because God "puts" righteousness on those that trust alone in the Savior.

That may not mean too much to skeptics and atheists right now, but on Judgment Day they will suddenly see that the Christian is free from the demands of the Law. It can't touch him. He is right with the Law, and the Scriptures even say that he can have "boldness" on the Day of Wrath. The Christian escapes execution. Death can't touch him. He has escaped the damnation of Hell.

That righteousness will come to you the moment you confess and forsake your sins. You will be born again, and God will give you a new heart with new desires. So, what are you waiting for?

Set aside your questions, your arguments, and your doubts, and humbly and earnestly call upon the name of the Lord. Go on. You may not have tomorrow. Time is ticking, and it will eventually take you into eternity. It may happen in time, or in the lack of a heartbeat.

The moment you find the truth of what I have just told you you will join the ranks of those who look upon that sacrifice—that old rugged cross—that bloodied torture stake, with new eyes. You will find a place of genuine godly sorrow, heartfelt humility, and unspeakable gratitude for such amazing grace…for the gift of eternal life.

CHAPTER FIFTEEN

BIRD BRAIN

"Ray, Birds and all animals are most certainly impressive,
no doubt. I have often sat in contemplation like that myself.
I just come to a different conclusion to you. Ever wonder
what goes on in the mind of a bird?"

YES. ALMOST every time I look at them. How do they know how and when to build a nest? How do they choose who to hang with? How do they recognize old friends (they all look the same)? Why don't we see fat sparrows? What are they singing about? Who teaches them music? How come they can all sing on key? How do they know that they are sparrows so that they can hang with other sparrows? Birds of a feather do flock together (how many sparrows do you see flying with seagulls?). Are they nervous on their first flight? Who warns them about cats? If it's their mom and dad, how do they communicate with their kids? Do they dream? What do they dream about? Cats? If they think, do they think in English or Chirp? Probably Chirp. Are they taught language skills while in the nest or afterwards at some sort of hidden Chirp school? Does the language have a similar structure to human language? When they all get together for a sing-along (we often hear loud tree choirs), do they have a conductor?

Is anyone is charge, or is it just a jam session of golden oldies?

As an atheist it must be a little frustrating having no one to thank for all this. How can you not stand in awe at the intelligence of the mind that put all this together? I marvel at the genius of God. Einstein did. Newton did. You don't. You see the meal but you never taste it…because you don't want to. What a tragedy.

We have a birdfeeder by a window in our living room where I do most of my writing. Every day I watch birds feeding, fluttering, fighting, and then flying off. But, as a Christian, I can't help but think deeper about what I witness every day. Each one of these little creatures is an amazingly made independent flying machine. I have read the biography of the Wright brothers and was fascinated by the fact that they continually studied principles of flight that they saw in birds before they constructed their own flying machine. We have the miracle of flight now because the Wright brothers copied God's handiwork. They watched as birds twisted their wings in flight and how they used their tails as rudders. If God hadn't given the Wright brothers clues though His creation, we would probably still be grounded today.

I watch these little birds land in a tiny space with absolute precision, flutter their amazingly made wings, and move their heads with incredibly delicate movements. Each one has its own personality, and a mind to feed on that which will benefit it. It has a memory of where the food is, and instinctively mixes with birds of its own kind, but its tiny eyes are peeled for cats. One cat or the movement of my hand and a dozen of them will leave in an instant. They don't panic at the first sign of danger and fly into each other, but in a split second they fly away in amazing unison. It's not as if one of them sounds an alarm and they leave. It's an instantaneous exit.

Each bird has a tiny brain, muscles that move the tail and twist the wings, a thirst, a hunger, an instinct to build a home, to start a family, to daily search for food, and to snooze at night. Each has a brain that coordinates tiny feet, wings, a stomach, digestive juices, lungs that pull in air, kidneys, bowels, a liver, blood, and a pumping heart that sends it and oxygen through the tiny brain that keeps each little bird alive and kicking.

How blind we are to the absolute genius of God. It grieves me that I can go through life and look at any part of creation and not be awed speechless by God's amazing hand. But I did that for twenty-two years of my unsaved life. I was a blind man, unaware that there was anything outside my own dark little world. What is even more grievous is that sinful man denies God due praise for His wonderful creation.

THE UNANSWERED PRAYER OF THE ATHEIST

The atheist has a problem with both answered and unanswered prayer. Here's a scenario that no doubt happens daily somewhere in the world. A young boy becomes deathly ill. The entire family gathers for prayer. However, despite earnest and sincere prayer, the child tragically dies. Their explanation for the death is that God took him to heaven because He wanted the child there. That's seen by the atheist as "unanswered prayer." Or the child miraculously makes a recovery, which the family hails as an evident miracle. God obviously answered the family's prayers by saving the child from death. The atheist maintains that it wasn't answered prayer but that the child recovered because his body healed itself.

Was the recovery a miracle? Perhaps. Then again, perhaps it wasn't. Only God knows. The fact is that we have no idea what happened. However, one thing we do know is that answered or unanswered prayer has nothing to do with God's existence. Let me explain. My wife has a Dodge Caravan. Let's say it has a problem. What would be my intellectual capacity if I concluded that it had no manufacturer simply because I couldn't contact them about the dilemma? The fact of their existence has nothing to do with whether or not they return my calls.

Neither does God's existence have anything to do with the fact that there are those who have experienced miracles, seen visions, or supposedly heard His voice. The sun doesn't exist because we see its light, or because we feel its warmth. Its existence has nothing to do with any human testimony. Nor does it cease to exist because a blind man is not aware of its reality, or because it becomes cloudy, or the night falls. The sun exists, period.

> *The sun doesn't exist because we see its light, or because we feel its warmth. Its existence has nothing to do with any human testimony. The sun exists, period.*

God's existence isn't dependent on the Bible or its authenticity, the existence of the church, the prophets, or even creation. God existed before the Scriptures were written, before creation came into existence. Even if the Bible were proved to be fraudulent, God would still exist.

Adamant atheist April Pedersen writes, "The human trait of seeking comfort through prayer is a strong one." This is true. However, April fails to see that human nature itself is very predictable. If men will not embrace the biblical revelation of God, their nature is to go into idolatry. "Idolatry" is the act of creating a god in our image, whether it is shaped with the human hands (a physical "idol"), or shaped in the human mind through the imagination. Those who create their own god then use it as a "good-luck charm" to do their bidding. The idolater uses his god for his own ends. He calls on his god to win a football game, a boxing match, the lottery, and, of course, to win a war. Idolatry is as predictable as it is illogical.

EVOLUTION AND THE BEGINNING

Zoologists have recorded an amazing twenty thousand species of fish. Each of theses species has a two-chambered heart that pumps cold blood throughout its cold body.

There are six thousand species of reptiles. They also have cold blood, but theirs is a three-chambered heart (except for the crocodile, which has four). The one thousand or so different amphibians (frogs, toads, and newts) have cold blood and a three-chambered heart.

There are over nine thousand different species of birds. From the massive Andean Condor with its wingspan of twelve feet to the tiny hummingbird (whose heart beats fourteen hundred times a minute), each of those nine thousand different species has a heart and blood. There are four chambers in their heart: the left atrium, the right atrium, the left ventricle, and the right ventricle—just like in a human.

Of course the fifteen thousand species of mammals have a pumping four-chambered heart that faithfully pumps blood throughout a series of intricate blood vessels to the rest of the body.

There are also a million named species of insects, and scientists estimate that there could be another million waiting to be discovered and named. All these different insects have an "open circulatory" system. Their blood flows from the blood vessels out the end into the body cavity. It swishes around the body cavity until it gets sucked back by the heart into the other open end of the blood system somewhere else. This is in contrast to mammals where the blood never leaves the blood vessels at any stage.

Here's an interesting question or two for the thinking evolutionist. Can you explain which came first (the blood or the heart) and why? Did the heart in all these different species of fish, reptiles, birds, amphibians, and insects evolve before there were blood vessels throughout their bodies? When did the blood evolve? Was it before the vessels evolved or after they evolved?

If it was before, what was it that carried the blood to the heart, if there were no vessels? Did the heart beat before the blood evolved? Why was it beating if there was no blood to pump? If it wasn't beating, why did it start when it didn't know anything about blood?

If the blood vessels evolved before there was blood, why did they evolve if there was no such thing as blood? And if the blood evolved before the heart evolved, what was it that kept it circulating around the body?

WHICH CAME FIRST?

The following are some attempts (by believers in evolution) to answer the question about which came first—the blood, the heart, or the blood vessels, and why:

> "Which came first? Blood (albeit in a different form), I'd guess. Why? I don't know."

> "Would you really listen to an explanation? It would be a lengthy one and I fear I couldn't avoid using big names such as 'coelom' or 'deuterostomia.'"

> "The concept of oxygen transporting molecules is much older than any kind of blood vessels."

> "No one needs evolution to show that you are out in left field with your irrational belief system."

"That is a very common tactic…. Ask a series of questions that would take two years of formal study to answer. And you expect to answer it in a blog comment."

"Those are questions for an evolutionary biologist…"

"Get real, Ray."

"As I understand it, blood came first, then blood vessels, then the heart."

"All you need is a little imagination, Ray. But I will not go there. It would require too much space."

"Ask them expecting an answer. Don't ask them expecting to catch people in a lie. You might learn something."

"I don't know how circulatory systems evolved. I'll go down to the local university and ask a biologist about it."

"You have a tendency to oversimplify scientific positions and ideas to the point where they become gross misrepresentations of the original idea, especially when these ideas are repeated by people who post on your blog who are not experts in the subject."

"Biology is not my science. So, I'm not the person to answer your question."

"I'd give you an answer, but I fear my cat will get more use out of it than you would, Ray."

"Maybe if you used the Internet for it's original purpose, you might *gasp* learn something."

The only answer to these questions is that Almighty God supernaturally made the human body (and every other creature) with a heart, lungs (needed for oxygenated blood), kidneys (to get rid of bad blood), vessels, arteries, blood, skin (to hold it all in), etc., all at once. Unthinkable for an atheist, but true.

I recently read the biography of Abraham Lincoln. It was written in Lincoln's own words, based on historical records. As I turned each page, I wondered how they would handle his assassination because he didn't say anything after he was shot in the head. In the book, he spoke of the grief of the Civil War, about how good it was to have peace back in the country, and how he went to a play with his wife. It was a comedy, so he spoke about how it was good to hear people laugh again. He said, "...to be with Mary...to think of the years ahead. Please God, never let people forget the joy of love, the pleasure of laughter, and the beauty of peace." Then there was simply a bold headline that read: "WASHINGTON, D.C. —President Abraham Lincoln was shot at Ford's Theater shortly after ten o'clock last evening. At 7:22 this morning, April 15, 1865, he died."

As I read those words, tears ran down my cheeks. I couldn't believe my reaction. I knew it was coming, so why was I crying like a child? This is why. Throughout the book, I got to know Abraham Lincoln, not as a cold historical figure but as a man with fears and pains. I grieved when his beloved sister suddenly died in her youth. I grieved with him at the loss of two of his children through sickness. The book personalized him to a point where I personally felt the pain of his untimely death.

Did you know that every twenty-four hours 150,000 people die? That's a lot of people. It makes us raise an eyebrow. But because it is just a cold statistic, it can wash over us like water on a dead duck's back. If we are going to have a passion for the unsaved, we have to personalize ourselves with them to a point where it brings more than a tear to our eye. We have to see those 150,000 people as moms and dads, sons and daughters, brothers and sisters...people with the same fears and pains we possess.

That is what is known as "empathy"—a virtue of compassion that causes us to feel the pain of another. "And on some have compassion, making a distinction; but others save with fear, pulling them out of the fire, hating even the garment defiled by the flesh" (Jude 1:22-23).

I found the following quote in an interesting article:[1]

> On Tuesday evening I attended the debate between Richard Dawkins and John Lennox at Oxford's Natural History Museum. This was the second public encounter between the two men, but it turned out to be very different from the first…This week's debate, however, was different because from the off, Dawkins moved it onto safer territory—and at the very beginning made a most startling admission. He said: "A serious case could be made for a deistic God."
>
> This was surely remarkable. Here was the arch-apostle of atheism, whose whole case is based on the assertion that believing in a creator of the universe is no different from believing in fairies at the bottom of the garden, saying that a serious case can be made for the idea that the universe was brought into being by some kind of purposeful force. A creator. True, he was not saying he was now a deist; on the contrary, he still didn't believe in such a purposeful founding intelligence, and he was certainly still saying that belief in the personal God of the Bible was just like believing in fairies. Nevertheless, to acknowledge that "a serious case could be made for a deistic god" is to undermine his previous categorical assertion that "…all life, all intelligence, all creativity and all 'design' anywhere in the universe is the direct or indirect product of Darwinian natural selection… Design cannot precede evolution and therefore cannot underlie the universe.'"

The God of the Old Testament

Richard Dawkins refers to "The God of the Old Testament" as a "megalomaniacal, sadomasochistic, capriciously malevolent bully." However, the God of the New Testament is just as offensive to the ungodly as the God of the Old Testament, because they are One in the same. He never changes. Jesus warned to fear Him because He had the power "to cast body and soul into Hell" (see Matthew 10:28).

Look at His terrible New Testament judgments: He killed a husband and wife simply because they told one lie (see Acts 5:1-11). His "wrath" abides on every unbeliever for their sins (see John 3:36, Ephesians 5:6). He will punish the unsaved with a fearful "indignation and wrath, tribulation and anguish" (Romans 2:8-9), and warns that He is going to be "revealed from Heaven with His mighty angels, in flaming fire taking vengeance on those who do not know God, and on those who do not obey the gospel of our Lord Jesus Christ" (see 2 Thessalonians 1:8).

He is so angry at this world He calls us His enemy (see James 4:4) and promises to "shake not only the earth, but also Heaven" in His wrath (Hebrews 12:26). Our God is "a consuming fire" (see Hebrews 12:29) and His justice will cause some to gnaw their tongues in pain (see Revelation 16:10). He is so serious about sin He will cast all liars into the lake of fire (see Revelation 21:8).

If you still want to paint the Old Testament God as being mean and the New Testament God as being nice, please realize that the God of the New Testament proclaimed the death sentence on every man, on every woman, and on every child of the human race. Every single human being will die because they have violated God's Law (see Romans 5:12, 6:23).

So the two Gods scenario is imaginary, and He isn't a "Megalomaniacal, sadomasochistic, capriciously malevolent bully," but an utterly perfect, holy, and righteous Creator. He will see that absolute justice is done on what the Bible calls "the Day of Wrath." That is what is offensive to guilty sinners. They are at enmity with God's Law (see Romans 8:7). They hate His moral government.

However, the same God of the Bible (who in the Old Testament said to love your neighbor as much as you love yourself (see Leviticus 19:18), is rich in mercy. He provided a way for us (in the New Testament) to be saved from His just wrath. This was through the blood of the Cross. If we refuse His offer of mercy, we will have to stand before His fearful justice. The New Testament warns, "It is a fearful thing to fall into the Hands of the Living God" (see Hebrews 10:31) and further adds "How shall we escape if we neglect so great a salvation?"

HOW'S YOUR WORD KNOWLEDGE?

I wonder if you know what the word *vicarious* means. It's an adjective that means that something is "endured or done by one person substituting for another: vicarious punishment." It's probably meaningless to an unsaved person. Few have had someone take their punishment for them. However, it means everything to the Christian. The saved person knows that he was once a lawbreaker—a devious criminal in the eyes of a holy God. He knows that God's standard of righteousness is so high that the crime of lying demands the death sentence and that He considers hatred of another human being to be murder. If you hate someone, as far as God is concerned you are physically putting a knife into his back. If you lust after another human being, God considers you to be an adulterer. That's the height of His moral standard, and that will be the standard of judgment on Judgment Day.

However, this same wrath-filled God is rich in mercy to all that call upon Him. He was manifest in the flesh and suffered for us so that we could be free from the demands of eternal justice. His was a "vicarious" sacrifice. He paid the fine so that God could legally dismiss our case. Then He rose again on the third day, and all who repent and trust in Jesus receive remission of sins. They are forgiven and washed clean of their filthiness. God grants them the gift of everlasting life. How do you know if this is true? Obey the Gospel "and you will know the truth and the truth will make you free" (see John 8:31-32).

I sat next to an intellectual on a plane recently. He was involved in the financial side of a well-known national corporation. I knew that he was pretty intelligent when I asked him a few questions just to fill in time and he answered them correctly. The first was, "How many U.S. presidents are not buried in the United States?" At that time there were four. They were Jimmy Carter, George Bush Senior, George Bush Junior, and Bill Clinton (although time will change the answer). The second was, "What was the highest mountain on earth before Mount Everest was discovered?" He knew that it was Mount Everest. It's always been the highest. He was one sharp cookie.

All other religions are what are called 'works-righteousness' religions. They think that they have to do something to earn everlasting life.

When I asked Joe what he thought happens after someone dies, he said that he wasn't an atheist, but that he didn't believe in an afterlife. There was no Heaven and no Hell. So was that the end of the conversation? Where can it go if someone doesn't believe in Heaven or Hell? There is a way. I asked Joe to imagine that there is a Heaven and asked if he thought that he was good enough to go there. Did he think that he was a good person? The conversation went like this:

"I'm a very good person."

"Let's go through some of the Commandments to see if you are, and if you will make it to Heaven. How many lies have you told in your life?"

It turned out that he was a liar, a thief, and a blasphemer, and that he had committed adultery in his heart many times. I explained the cross, the necessity of repentance and faith, and thanked him for listening to me.

About thirty minutes later he started up the conversation again: "I have a question for you. Why is it that Christianity says that people from all other religions are going to Hell?"

"All other religions are what are called 'works-righteousness' religions. They think that they have to do something to earn everlasting life. The Muslim prays five times a day, fasts, etc. The Hindu fasts, prays, lies on beds of nails, etc. The thing that changes the equation is God's Law. It shows us that we are not simply unfortunate human beings trying to make our way through this life, but that we are wicked criminals in the sight of a holy God. So our 'good' works suddenly are not good works, but are actually attempts to bribe the Judge of the Universe. And the Bible warns that "the sacrifice of the wicked is an abomination to the Lord." He will not be bribed. But in Christianity, God provided a way for all humanity—the Muslim, the Hindu, the Buddhist, the Jew, and the Gentile to be saved. The offer of everlasting life is come by the mercy of the Judge—as a free gift. It is universal—'whosoever will,' may come."

Joe thought for a moment, and said, "I don't accept that. It seems unfair to me that it is exclusive."

"You mean that Jesus said that He was the only way to God?"

"Yes."

"Do you think that Christianity is 'intolerant?'"

"Yes, I do."

"So you are being intolerant of Christianity? You are doing what you are accusing Christianity of doing. Being intolerant."

"No, no, not at all. I was just wondering…"

For the next hour or so, Joe had many questions. He listened thoughtfully and took a "What Hollywood Believes" CD and a copy of *The Way of the Master New Testament*. At the end of the flight he thanked me for the conversation and said that he had learned a lot.

When he said that he didn't believe in Heaven and Hell it seemed like a dead end. So, if someone doesn't believe, surmise with them for a moment. Have them imagine that there's a Heaven (it's easy if you try), and it will open up a door to their heart. Always remember that you are dealing with those that the Bible says are blind. You want them to know that there is another world, so speak to their God-given imagination, and that will give you the opportunity to speak to their God-given conscience.

CHAPTER SIXTEEN

RIGHT ON THE MONEY

T O SEE HOW precise Scripture is in its prediction, consider the claims made in 2 Peter 3:3-9:

1. There would be scoffers in the last days (preceding the Second Coming).

2. They would say that the signs of the Second Coming have always been around.

3. They would deny the Noahic worldwide flood (despite overwhelming scientific evidence).

4. Their specific sin would be "lust."

5. God is waiting for them to repent, because it's not His will that they go to Hell.

6. Their error is that they think that God is subject to the dimension of time.

[K]nowing this first: that scoffers will come in the last days, walking according to their own lusts, and saying,

"Where is the promise of His coming? For since the fathers fell asleep, all things continue as they were from the beginning of creation." For this they willfully forget: that by the word of God the heavens were of old, and the earth standing out of water and in the water, by which the world that then existed perished, being flooded with water. But the heavens and the earth which are now preserved by the same word, are reserved for fire until the day of judgment and perdition of ungodly men. But, beloved, do not forget this one thing, that with the Lord one day is as a thousand years, and a thousand years as one day. The Lord is not slack concerning His promise, as some count slackness, but is longsuffering toward us, not willing that any should perish but that all should come to repentance" (2 Peter 3:3-9).

Some years ago a friend flew me to Israel. After visiting Jericho, we boarded a bus and made our way back through the mountainous passes toward Jerusalem. I was sitting right up in the front of a large bus, on the right side, while the rest of the group sat more toward the back.

The road was very narrow, with a deep valley on the right-hand side. As we approached a very sharp left turn in the road, the driver slowed down, moved toward the right of the road, then swung the steering wheel around the corner. The result was that my part of the bus went right over the edge of the road as we slowly turned. It was just then that I made the mistake of looking out of the window. My part of the bus was suspended over the edge as we turned, and I looked down in horror at a three-thousand-foot drop into the deep valley below. For about two seconds I was sure that I was going to die.

Suddenly it was over, and we were merrily driving along the road. The driver and rest of the passengers were totally oblivious as to what I had just experienced. I sat there in disbelief and humbly thanked God that I was still alive. In a matter of two seconds, I had gained a new appreciation for my precious life.

Even at this moment, I still benefit profoundly from that terrifying experience. I am forever thankful for the gift of life, and my gratitude is directed at God alone.

The Moral Law hangs us over eternity. For those of us who experience true conviction of sin, it is an overwhelming horror. The reality of our depravity demands that we be damned forever. We look around at the rest of humanity and see that they are oblivious to what is happening. Life is a joyride, and death and damnation are far from their thoughts. But for us, the Law calls for our execution. It stirs a conscience that points its finger at our guilt. We are going to be damned, and there's no hope. None. The experience takes our breath away in horror.

But then we hear of the Cross—the glorious good news of the Cross! Jesus Christ suffered and died for us, while we were yet sinners. We hear that God has turned a corner for humanity through the Gospel. We can live—forever. Oh the relief of God's mercy! Oh the unspeakable gratitude that suddenly comes from nowhere and explodes toward God for His kindness.

Without the terrors of the Law, the professed Christian drives along the path of life with no appreciation for what we have been given in the Gospel. That's why so many within the church can sit passively in the pew. They have never experienced the terrors of the Law and so they don't have gratitude enough to even consider doing the will of the God they profess to love.

GRASPING FOR EVIDENCE

"I'm intrigued that you say paintings and watches are bound by the laws of nature when the Bible talks of parting seas, walking on water, healing without medicine, random, global flooding, smiting, pillars of salt, virgin birth, resurrection and more—none of which seem to obey any laws of nature we've discovered to date."

This epitomizes the problem of speaking with a professing atheist. They stand on their own oxygen hose, and then wonder why they are grasping for evidence of the existence of God. However, what they maintain that they cannot find—evidence—is right in front of their nose. God created the sea. It didn't crawl up out of a puddle billions of years ago, created by nothing. How crazy is that? So, if God made the sea, He can part it if He wants to. If He made the sea, He can also walk on it. If He created the human body, He can fix it when it breaks. He can smite what he wants, when He wants. He can create pillars of salt, pillars of fire, and pillars of goose feathers, if He wants. Virgin birth? No problem. Resurrection—piece of cake (see Acts 26:8).

The problem is, we are trying to reason with the person the Bible calls a "fool" (see Psalm 14:1) and fools tend to be very unreasonable.

Did you know that proof of evolution has been right under our noses all this time? We have finally found the missing link. The tadpole *evolves* into the frog in a matter of weeks ("Fish Gets Legs").

Of course, a true evolutionist believes that the tadpole isn't a true fish.

The caterpillar evolves into the butterfly ("Bug Gets Wings"). God speeds up the process from millions of years to just twenty-one days, so that you can actually see the transition.

Speaking of transitions—God has set a Day in which He will judge the world in righteousness. If you have lusted, you have committed adultery in His sight. If you have hated anyone, you are a murderer, according to the Bible. You need a Savior—someone who can save you from the wrath of the Law you have violated.

Fortunately (understatement of eternity), God has provided One to save us from Hell. Jesus suffered on the Cross, taking the punishment for our sins. We broke the Law, and Jesus paid our fine. That's love! Then He rose from the dead and defeated death, and now God can forgive us. He can dismiss our case if we will repent and trust in Jesus Christ. What a wonderful deal. How kind God is to us rebellious sinners.

AN ATHEIST'S QUESTION

"Name one feature about humanity that can be demonstrated as unique." Atheism. Only human beings have the ability to bow the knee and worship the God that gave them life. Only human beings have the ability to deny His evident existence. We are utterly unique among God's creation because He has made us in His image.

WE ARE APES. SURE.

"We are apes. If there is such thing as a God, and if such God made us to his image, well, he obviously made the other apes to his image too."

God *did* make man in His image, and He made male and female so that they could reproduce after their own kind. Evolution believers erroneously believe that all of creation (millions of kinds), *by themselves*, came into being as male and female, and then gave themselves the ability to reproduce after their own kind.

The difference between man and apes is that man is a moral being. If you don't believe it, watch the comments on this blog and see how moral atheists point to the Moral Law to say that I have deviated morally from the truth (see Exodus 20:16).

What's more, God made man as a man. He created sheep as they are—as sheep. He created birds, and fish as they are—as birds and fish. They were "in the beginning" as they are now. Nothing evolved and nothing is evolving. Tadpoles still change into frogs and caterpillars still change into butterflies, and they do that because God made them that way, not because of evolution.

About the God You Don't Believe In

"Let's be a bit more realistic and say that it takes God half an hour to bring every idle sin into the light. Then it would take 4.278 million years to judge mankind in its entirety. Each year God could judge 525,960 persons (and bring all their sins into the light). That means: if the 75 billion humans who are to be judged could maintain a population growth of 0.00070128% a year they would outbreed all of God's judging efforts."

I have to answer you saying the same words that Jesus said to the naïve skeptics of His day: "Jesus answered and said to them, 'Are you not therefore mistaken, because you do not know the Scriptures nor the power of God?'" (Mark 12:24). I know that you don't believe in a Creator, but bear with me for a moment while I try and reason with you.

You and I are standing on this huge ball, spinning at over a thousand miles per hour, and screaming through space at an incredible sixty-seven thousand miles per hour. Almighty God spoke it into existence in an instant. He made millions of fish and birds, insects, animals, and mankind, all with eyes, ears, brains, and individual instincts to survive and reproduce.

He sees every thought of every human heart. He hears every word of every mouth that passes the teeth, the tongue, and the taste buds He made. He sees every atom He created. Nothing is hidden from His holy eyes. He even knows how many hairs are on your head. He made every one of them. Where do you think they came from? If you think that they happened by accident, or there was nothing in the beginning that created everything, then you make one hair from nothing, and I will be first to fall at your feet and worship you. But you will get more than my adulation. You will get the adoration of millions (and make a billion dollars overnight), because all the bald guys that look daily at their hairless heads will give an arm and a leg just to have some hair that you can so easily make.

The image of the god you don't believe in is erroneous. It truly is an "image" that sits in your fertile image-ination. The true God is nothing like what you conceive Him to be. He can judge the entire race in an instant of time ("time" is His creation), just as He brought about this earth and all that dwell on it in a moment of time.

So stop the mockery and get on your knees. Humble your proud heart, confess, and forsake your many sins and trust the Savior. Or you will have to face Him on what the Bible calls the "Day of Wrath," and my feeble words can't express how fearful that will be.

WHAT'S THE BIG DEAL?

"Psalm 103 Verse 12 states: 'As far as the east is from the west, so far hath he removed our transgressions from us.' What does that verse mean on a spherical world?! There is neither "a east" nor "a west" on our planet. Does God know, when we repent, remove our sins so far eastwards/westwards from us, that they will be again with us? I mean if you go on a spherical world as far east as possible you will end up just where you started…"

When I first read this I thought that you had become a Christian. That's because this is a wonderful faith-building and consoling promise for every believer. Thank you for bringing it up.

Before I was a Christian I did some things of which I am now very ashamed. I was extremely ungrateful. In twenty-two years of my godless existence, I didn't think seriously for two minutes about the God who gave me life. I was a selfish, godless, and lust-filled wretch, and didn't even know it until I looked at His Moral Law. I was blind, foolish, and unwittingly on my way to Hell. But through the Cross, God forgave me a multitude of sins.

However, He more than just forgave me. He removed my sins (as you have so kindly pointed out) "as far as the East is from the West." What does that mean? How far is the East from the West?

Picture the earth. If you were located at any point on the globe and began to travel in a northerly direction, eventually you would round the North Pole and then be traveling south. Likewise, if you were located at any point on the globe and then began to travel in a southerly direction, eventually you would round the South Pole and then be traveling north.

However, the distance from the East to the West can't be calculated. It is impossible to measure. You can travel in an easterly direction for a million miles and you will never find a point at which East and West touch. Mathematicians refer to the distance between East and West as "infinity." The two can never meet. "Oh, East is East, and West is West, and never the twain shall meet, till earth and sky stand presently at God's great Judgment Seat..." says poet Rudyard Kipling.

Perhaps you are thinking, "So what's the big deal?" Imagine you committed adultery, and afterward you are utterly broken by what you have done. You are guilt-ridden at your betrayal of trust, and so you confess your sin to your faithful wife. She is filled with nothing but love and grace and says that she will not only forgive you, but she promises that she will forget what you did. The problem is, as a human being, you know that she can never "forget" while she is in a sane mind. But God can…because He is God.

He says that He has cast my many transgressions into the sea of His forgetfulness. He has blotted out my sins and removed them from me "as far as the East is from the West," and that means even the weight of guilt has gone.

As soon as Adam sinned, his guilt caused him to try and hide from God. That's what the professing atheist does in his mind. He lives in denial of the existence of the One he has sinned against. In truth, his guilt makes him run from God as a criminal runs from the law. Atheism is the ultimate delusion.

Instead, turn around and face God. Repent as you would if you had committed adultery and you wanted your wife's forgiveness. Then trust the Savior and you will find that you no longer want to run from Him. Your guilt will be removed in an instant and you will come to know the One who has already dealt with your sins. And He will give you a new heart with new desires. Even as I write this, there are tears of gratitude in my eyes. Join me.

Each of us is bound by moral absolutes whether he knows it or not, just as he is bound by the law of gravity, whether he knows it or not. A criminal may steal a car and drive dangerously on a freeway as the law chases him, but his pleading ignorance will not exonerate him from civil law. He clocks up its wrath every time he transgresses its precepts. The same happens every time you violate God's Law. Each time you lie, steal, lust, fornicate, commit adultery, or blaspheme, you are storing up the Law's wrath, and God will see to it that you get exactly what you deserve on the Day of Judgment.

If you are an atheist, you don't believe that. Otherwise you would be a Christian. You are like a man who says that the law of gravity has no influence over him at all. He jumps from the tenth floor to show you, and as he passes the third floor he calls, "See, I'm flying." He's right. He is flying. But he will eventually suffer the terrible consequences of his foolishness.

Science discovered that when a certain object moves at a certain speed, it supersedes the law of gravity and can fly. If we could go back five hundred years in time, almost every thinking scientist would have said that such talk is utterly foolish. He would have maintained that it was impossible for an object the size of a 747 jumbo jet to fly like a bird. However, we now know that even though the law of gravity remains, the flying object has moved into a higher law, the invisible law of aerodynamics.

Ignorant people mock the fact that the Christian has discovered a higher law than the law of sin and death. Their thought is that everyone dies, not knowing that there's another law of which the Bible speaks. Listen to what the Apostle Paul said: "The law of life in Christ Jesus has made me free from the law of sin and death" (Romans 8:2). I know that you are different than the normal atheist. Take no notice of the ignorant scoffers. Please, open your mind and soften your heart. There's so much more out there (in the realm of the invisible) than we can begin to imagine.

By the way, you will never see that your ways are perverse until you (with a tender conscience) judge yourself by the perfect standard of God's Moral Law. How about you take some time to carefully read the Sermon on the Mount (Matthew Chapters 5-7), and give me your thoughts?

"He who walks in his uprightness fears the Lord, but he who is perverse in his ways despises Him" (Proverbs 14:2).

CHAPTER SEVENTEEN

WHAT REALLY MATTERS

*"Ray, I have a question for you. I am getting frustrated
having to try and 'prove' God's existence day in and day out
to unbelievers all the time. Do I really need to 'prove' God to
anyone or just preach the gospel? I don't see why I should
have to 'prove' what God has already said in His word.
I'd love some advice on how you handle this."*

WE DON'T have to prove that God exists to the professing atheist. This is because he intuitively knows that He exists. Every person has a God-given conscience. The Bible tells us that this is the "work of the law written on their hearts." Just as every sane human being knows that it's wrong to lie, steal, kill, and commit adultery, he knows that God should be first in his life.

The professing atheist not only has the testimony of his impartial conscience, but he also has the testimony of creation. It "declares" the glory of God, and the person who denies the voice of conscience and the voice of creation is without excuse. If death seizes upon him and he is still in his sins, he will face the wrath of a holy Creator, whether he believes in Him or not.

This is why I don't spend too much time trying to convince anyone that there is a God. To do so is to waste time and energy. What sinners need isn't to be convinced that God exists, but that sin exists and that they are in terrible danger. The only biblical way to do this is to go through the Moral Law and explain that God considers lust to be adultery and hatred to be murder, etc. It is the revelation that God is holy and just, and sees the thought-life that convinces us that we are in danger of eternal damnation. That's what sent me to the Cross for mercy and that's what sinners need to hear. So never be discouraged from preaching the Gospel, and don't get sidetracked by the rabbit trails of issues that don't really matter.

THE ABSURDITY OF CHRISTIANITY

"I would like to ask you a couple of relevant questions pertaining to the 'sacrifice' of Jesus and its purpose. Please logically explain why an omnipotent, omniscient, and omni-benevolent God would need to sacrifice Himself (as Jesus) to Himself (God) in order to forgive man of sins against Him (God)? The entire premise seems totally absurd."

I appreciate the way you said that the sacrifice of the cross seems absurd. It does. The Bible is in agreement with you: "For the message of the cross is foolishness to those who are perishing, but to us who are being saved it is the power of God" (1 Corinthians 1:18). There's good reason that it seems absurd.

Imagine if I said to you, "I just sold my house and my car, and used all my savings to pay a fine for you." You would understandably think that I am rather weird. My paying a fine for you, when you don't think you have done anything wrong, is absurd.

But if I put it this way it may make more sense: "Chuck, angry police officers showed up with a warrant for your arrest. They have video of you going 80 mph through an area set aside for a blind children's convention. There were clear warning signs everywhere saying that 15 mph was the maximum speed. You are in big trouble. Add to that the fact that just ten minutes prior to that happening, they stopped you for drunk driving and confiscated your driver's license. You were in serious trouble with the law. The judge was furious, and handed down a massive fine. He said that if you couldn't pay it, you were going to be thrown in prison for a very long time. I knew you didn't have any money, so I sold my house and my car, and I used all my savings to pay that fine. You are free to go."

The reason you think the fine being paid for you two thousand years ago is absurd is because you don't realize that you have seriously broken the Moral Law (the Ten Commandments) and you are in big trouble (see 1 John 3:4). In your drunken atheistic stupor you have ignored the clear warning signs of your violated conscience and you have sped with reckless abandon into sin. All the while, the video has been rolling. God is omnipresent and omniscient. He has seen your lust (see Matthew 5:27-28), fornication, lies, anger, blasphemy, and rebellion. He sees your thought life, and the darkness as if it were pure light (see Psalm 139:1-12). To say that He is angry at you is a massive understatement. His wrath abides on you (see John 3:36). You are His enemy (see James 4:4). Every time you sin against His Law, you are storing up His wrath (see Romans 2:5). Not believing that fact won't change a thing.

What sinners need isn't to be convinced that God exists, but that sin exists and that they are in terrible danger. The only biblical way to do this is to go through the Moral Law.

You could try and trivialize your crimes, but before you do, think of this. If I lied to my dog, it wouldn't be a big deal. If I was caught in a lie to my wife, I might have to spend the night on the couch. If I lied to my boss, I might lose my job. If I lied to a Supreme Court judge, I would spend a long time in prison. Even though it's the same crime, the penalty increases according to the importance of the one to whom I am lying.

All sin is against Almighty God (see Psalm 51:1-4). It is His Law that you have violated with your lust, lying, stealing, hatred, fornication, blasphemy, etc. You are as guilty as sin, and what's more you cannot justify (make things right) yourself.

So, how can your fine be paid? How about you offer all the gold, all the diamonds, or all the oil in the world? That won't work. It all belongs to God anyway. You have nothing to offer God as a payment. Nothing.

Think of the ancient Aztecs. They could see that they had angered their dozens of gods (the evident suffering, disease, and death), so they would try and appease them with a "payment." They would take the most precious thing they had—a handsome youth or a beautiful virgin—and they would sacrifice them on a bloody altar to try and make atonement. However, the Bible says that any sacrifice we make is an abomination to God. He strictly forbids human sacrifice. You may remember that He tested Abraham's love for Him by telling him to offer his only son. As he was about to sacrifice Isaac, God stopped him and then He provided the sacrifice. This was a foreshadow of God's sacrificing His only-begotten Son for the sin of the world). Besides being a murderous act, human sacrifice offers tainted sinful blood. It would be like me offering a judge drug money to pay your fine.

So what is precious enough to pay your fine and justify you so that you are free from the wrath of God's Law? Here's where the sacrifice makes sense.

As I have said, God Himself provided the sacrifice. Jesus was morally perfect. His blood wasn't tainted with sin like yours and mine—"[K]nowing that you were not redeemed with corruptible things, like silver or gold, from your aimless conduct received by tradition from your fathers, but with the precious blood of Christ, as of a lamb without blemish and without spot" (1 Peter 1:18-19). When He was on that terrible Cross, He was paying the fine for the Law that you and I violated (what love is that!).

Most people don't know that Jesus of Nazareth was Almighty God in human form. God prepared a body for Himself and filled that body as a hand fills a glove (see John 1:1, Colossians 1:15-16, 1 Timothy 3:16). The Creator was in Christ "reconciling the world to Himself."

One of the last things Jesus uttered on the Cross was, "It is finished!" (Actually, the English is inadequate; the better Greek rendering is, "The debt has been paid!") That now means that God can legally dismiss your case. He can commute your death sentence and let you live forever.

This was confirmed by the fact that God raised Jesus from the dead. It was God saying, "Humanity can now be justified."

This is why religious works (giving money to charities, praying five times a day, lying on beds of nails, or sitting on hard pews) cannot justify us. God will not be bribed (see Ephesians 2:8-9). The only thing that can save us from damnation (the just punishment for our sins) is the grace of God (unmerited favor—mercy from the judge), and that comes through repentance and faith (trust) alone in Jesus.

Some may ask why God didn't just simply forgive us. This is because He is *bound* by His own holy character. The Bible tells us that His Law is perfect, holy, just, and good. We are also told that *God* is perfect, holy, just, and good. So, we *cannot* separate God from His Law. It is His very essence. Scripture calls Him "the habitation of justice," and perfect justice *demands* retribution. That wrath-filled retribution fell on the Savior. If you refuse to repent, it will fall on you. Jesus warned that it would "grind to powder." When something is ground to powder, a *thorough* job is done. The Law will search out every sinful thought, word, and deed.

So there you have it. God loved you so much that He provided a sacrifice to save you from death and Hell. Call upon Him today, and He will save you. You have His immutable promise: "For the message of the cross is foolishness to those who are perishing, but to us who are being saved it is the power of God."

P.S. If it still seems absurd, read the last sentence through slowly, and try and figure out why.

AMAZING FACE

Have you ever objectively studied your face? There are billions of faces, and every one is different (except for "identical" twins). Each one has its own individual characteristics, and yet God made every one with just two eyes, a nose, and a mouth. If you think that's no big deal, try it yourself, from nothing.

Think about the ethnicity of each face. The Chinese look different from the Japanese and the Tibetans. The Dutch look different from the English and the German. You can pick a Russian from a Brazilian or someone from Africa, simply by looking at his face.

But the genius of Almighty God is even more wonderful. Look into the mirror and study your face closely. Start with no expression, and then see if you can act. Use your eyes only to express fear, pain, joy, disappointment, anger, thoughtfulness, and amazement. You won't be able to confine the emotion to the eyes. You will feel the muscles—particularly around your eyes and mouth automatically (with no conscious effort on your part) join in with whatever emotion you express through your eyes. The human face is much more than "amazing." It's a miracle of the unspeakable genius of the Creator. What an honor (understatement of eternity) to know Him, to love Him, and to serve Him.

Do you know Him? Or do you just know about Him? The way to come to know Him (in whom the Bible says dwells the source of life and light) is to think about your many sins and then think soberly about the Savior and what He did for you on the Cross. Then apologize to God, turn from that sin, and entrust yourself completely to the person of Jesus Christ. That's the way of salvation. It's so simple, a child can understand it. So what are you waiting for? Evidence? You need no more than a mirror. Face it.

THIS IS WHAT YOU ARE SAYING...

"I sometimes have trouble telling right from wrong. I just thought maybe we could work toward an America in which no one wants an abortion as opposed to making it illegal and having people get it anyway in very dangerous environments. That's just how I see it. I guess I do want it both ways. I want to be both pro-life in terms of my personal life and pro-choice in terms of how I vote."

I appreciate your honesty. However, this is in essence what you are saying, "I want a Germany in which no one wants to kill Jews as opposed to making it illegal and having them killed in very dangerous environments. I want to keep Jews alive in terms of my personal life and have them murdered in terms of how I vote." Nice.

Your "I sometimes have trouble telling right from wrong" pinpoints your problem. Atheism has no moral anchor. There's no absolute right or absolute wrong. That's why you can advocate murder and not feel bad about it, all in the name of compassion. In one sense, you may be right about not having a soul. So where is your conscience? Why have you so hardened it? If I were in your shoes I would very quickly cry out to God for His forgiveness, and trust Jesus Christ before it's too late. Once you know His mercy, and once you let His love into your cold heart, you will be horrified that any human being could sink so low as to advocate the killing of children in the womb.

SPECIES-TO-SPECIES DEFINITION

"'I have read most of Ray's books, seen most of his videos and heard hundreds of his witness encounters, and as of yet have never caught him in a lie.' Then you are willfully ignoring data. Mr. Comfort engages in demonstrable dishonesty when he makes mention of transitional fossil forms, as he misrepresents the meaning of transitional in the context of fossils."

I am often accused of lying, especially when it comes to saying that there are no "species-to-species" transitional forms. Before I explain what I mean, it's important to know that there is some confusion as to the meaning of the word "species." This is what the dictionary says of the word: "Biology: the major subdivision of a genus or subgenus, regarded as the basic category of biological classification, composed of related individuals that resemble one another, are able to breed among themselves, but are not able to breed with members of another species." Wolves, coyotes, and German shepherds are of the same species (the canine family or "kind"), but they can't breed with cats or tigers (which are the felidae family or "kind").

When I say there are no species-to-species transitional forms in the fossil record, I am saying that nowhere will you find a skeleton of a cat evolving into a dog, or a chicken evolving into a fish, or a horse into a cow, no matter how long you go back in history.

As the Bible so rightly says, every animal brings forth "after its own kind." In the creation we see around us (and in creation we see locked into the historical fossil record) is evidence against, not for, the theory of Darwinian evolution. All of nature screams of intelligent design. All of it. None even hints of Darwinian evolution. If you think that's a lie, then so be it.

THE GAME OF SPECULATION

"You seem firm in your beliefs that evolutionists claim that 'cows turn into dogs' and whatnot. So I'll make it simpler still for you: What characteristics would YOU expect to see in a transitional reptile/avian fossil? What characteristics of such a fossil would you accept to show evidence of a reptile becoming more birdlike?"

You are asking me to play the game that evolutionists play. It is the game of "Speculation." It uses a special language made up of words such as "perhaps," "maybe," etc. You may as well ask me to speculate on the signs that would be present for Cinderella's coach to be able to turn into a pumpkin. I don't believe in fairy tales and I don't believe in the unscientific theory of evolution. Reptiles don't turn into birds no matter how long you leave them. Every animal brings forth after its own kind, both in creation and in the fossil record. Chickens were not dinosaurs billions of years ago, despite the musings of evolutionary imagineers. I believe in true science, not the pseudo-science of evolution.

Also, I have never said that evolutionists believe that cows turn into dogs. I have said that there is no *scientific evidence* of any species "evolving" into another species. That's the evidence that is still missing.

You have your own definition of evolution, but ask the average person on the street what he believes it is, and he will say that Darwin said that man evolved from primates—that our great-great-great-grandfather was an ape. You believe in a common ancestor (like a branch on a tree of common descent); they don't. They believe that we are *direct* descendants, that we are apes. And who can blame them for the confusion when speculators like Richard Dawkins say things like, "We admit that we are like apes, but we seldom realize that we are apes—In truth, not only are we apes, we are African apes" ("Gaps in the Mind").

It is very clear that there is no empirical evidence for Darwinian evolution. Look at the last sentence in this quote about the supposed 47-million-year-old primate named Ida. It was unveiled as the missing link: "This will be the one pictured in the textbooks for the next hundred years," said Dr Jørn Hurum, the paleontologist from Oslo University's Natural History Museum who assembled the scientific team to study the fossil. "It tells a part of our evolution that's been hidden so far. It's been hidden because the only [other] specimens are so incomplete and so broken there's nothing almost to study."[1]

Notice what he said: "...ther specimens are so incomplete and so broken there's nothing almost to study." Drop the word "almost" and you have the truth. If you choose to blindly believe in evolution then you believe a lie (see Romans 1:25). Carl Sagan said, "We will not be afraid to speculate, but we will be careful to distinguish speculation from fact."[2] If you choose to believe the theory of evolution, you have failed to do that.

OPEN-MINDED EVOLUTIONIST

"Ray, do you call everyone who disagrees with you and posts a comment here an Atheist? That's a bit much. There could be quite a few individuals here who just want to set you straight on topics like evolution. Which does not make them an Atheist. I accept evolution and I believe in God and I am not alone. I for one would just like to see you open your mind and read some peer reviewed articles on the subject and try learn something instead of maligning science and spewing ignorance." J. G.

There is only one God and He revealed Himself—and how we were created—through His Word. In Scripture we are told that God made man in His own image. He created Adam as a man and then He created a female for him so he could reproduce after his own kind.

So the god that you believe in is what is known as an "idol." An idol is the creation of the human mind and is often then shaped with hands from wood or stone. The reason we are so prone to idolatry is that an idol doesn't tell us what to do. An idol doesn't consider lust to be adultery or hatred to be murder, and it doesn't condemn lying and stealing. An idol is dumb, and the Bible says those that create them are like them. We can shape our little god into anything we feel comfortable with, even if it's an unthinking and unscientific theory that we believe gives us a license to sin.

> *The reason we are so prone to idolatry is that an idol doesn't tell us what to do... We can shape our little god into anything we feel comfortable with.*

You are right about not being alone when it comes to idolatry. Millions worship false gods. You may not have formed your own religion with your god (Hinduism has 450 million gods), but he is extremely popular, especially in the Western world and among university students. And anyone who is gullible enough to believe in evolution will also be gullible enough to believe that when they create a god in their mind, it somehow does exist. Yet it doesn't. It's a figment of a fertile imagination (the place of imagery). Idolaters still have to face the God of the Bible on the Day of Judgment, whether they believe in Him or not.

Imagine that—standing alone before the throne of a holy and perfect Creator, the One that spoke the sun into existence and has seen every thought that has passed through your sinful mind. Imagine that—standing alone before Almighty God who requires an account of every idle word you have spoken, and every deed you have done, even if it is in secret. I think that you had better forget your image of god, repent, and trust in the Savior before it's too late.

GOOD FORNICATORS

We are a nation that has fallen away from God. Most believe in His existence and pray daily, but as the Bible says, we only have a "form" of godliness. According to bullypulpit@googlegroups.com, studies reveal that since 1970, the number of Americans living together has increased from about half a million opposite-sex couples to more than five million. That's ten million individual Americans, living in fornication.

A new analysis also found that the marriage rate is down in all countries except Norway and Sweden, which have had traditionally low marriage rates anyway. Meanwhile in the United States from 1995 to 2005, the marriage rate declined almost 20 percent.

A thirty-three-year-old Brooklyn woman has even co-authored a book called, *The Good Girl's Guide to Living in Sin*. She says that many women her age and younger view living with a romantic partner as a convenience and that it's not about avoiding marriage. She adds, "It's what's happening in the world of dating, and it's not necessarily a path anywhere." The woman is wrong about that—it is a "path" that leads somewhere. God's Word makes it clear that fornicators will not inherit the Kingdom of God.

The title of her book is interesting. Humanity has always messed with the word "good." A pedophile, a rapist, an adulterer, and even a mass murderer may think that they are morally good, and that may be true if the word "good" is relative. But it's not. The word "good" (in God's Book) is set in stone. It means to be morally perfect, in thought, word, and deed.

Most of us will continue to think that we are morally good, as long as we are ignorant of the perfect and holy standard by which God will judge us on Judgment Day.

As Christians, if we care about the people of this world, we must use the Moral Law to show them that they are in great error and desperately need His mercy.

HATING GOD

"Atheists don't hate any god, fairy, leprechaun, unicorn, or other fictional being. It's impossible to hate something that does not exist. Try to get this burned in your mind this time. Repeat it a few thousand times if that helps."

That's right. Atheists don't hate fairies, leprechauns, or unicorns, because they don't exist. It is impossible to hate something that doesn't exist. And that makes the point. You hate God because He does exist. You spend your time thinking about Him, then arguing about Him, then blaspheming His name and showing contempt for—and ridicule of—those that love Him. What greater hatred can you have for a person than to use his name as a cuss word?

You have the axiomatic evidence of creation and of your conscience, and you are therefore without excuse. By professing the blindness of atheism you are denying the God-given light that He has given each of us.

There are some cultures that will show so much contempt for a family member that has wronged them that they actually deny his existence. They refuse to acknowledge that he existed as a son. They don't want to see him, hear from him, or talk to him. That's what the professing atheist does with God, and his or her reason for doing so is moral. It's not intellectual. If it were an intellectual issue there wouldn't be any argument. But because you love your sins and you know that God requires an account for every action and every word (including your thought life), you can't stand that thought, and so you deny His existence.

THE "EMPTY" THREAT OF HELL

"The difference between the Bible and an instruction book is the myriad of untestable (and detestable) claims the Bible makes. How do you know that if I 'sin' I will go to Hell? Only from the Bible, which is a source of such dubious credibility as to be laughable. Can you prove to me that ANY of what the Bible claims about Hell and 'sin' is true? Can you prove to me that Hell exists? If not, you, along with all your pulpit-pounding ilk, are nothing more than a carnival ride of empty threats."

Hell is no empty threat. If I believed it was, I wouldn't bother warning you. However, the way for anyone who doesn't like the thought is to say that you don't believe in God. That cuts the problem off for you at the Source. All you have to do is ignore your God-given common sense. He doesn't exist because you don't believe in Him. You could carry this further if you didn't like gravity, history, the wind, or love. Those things can't be seen, and therefore wouldn't exist if you didn't believe in them either. Anything that you don't like will not exist if you just say that you don't believe in it.

The key to being a committed atheist is to be totally unreasonable. When someone denies the obvious, you can't reason with them. That's why you can be presented with the absolute and clear evidence of creation (which screams of a Creator to any reasonable person), and you can say that there's no evidence for God.

If you were reasonable, I would say that we know that Hell exists because we know intuitively that God is good. And if He is good, He must by nature punish a man who has tied up and raped three teenage girls, and then one by one, strangled them to death. In this case, justice delayed is not justice denied. God will bring that murderer to judgment and see that he gets exactly what he deserves, and Hell is the place of God's justice. It's His prison. Common sense tells that if God is good, it is right that He is also just. However, God is so good He will also punish thieves, liars, fornicators, adulterers, blasphemers, and everyone who has violated His perfect and holy Law. That leaves us all in big trouble. Without a Savior we will get exactly what we deserve, and that is a fearful thing.

It was evolutionist Professor Richard Lewontin who said, "The eminent Kant scholar Lewis Beck used to say that anyone who could believe in God could believe in anything." How true this is. With God, nothing is impossible.

No doubt Mr. Beck was rather thinking of the gullibility of human nature when he made his observation. It's true, people are easily conned, and the biggest con ever pulled over the eyes of humanity is the inane theory tale of Darwinian evolution. It is a lesson to us never to take what we are told on face value.

But the question must be asked as to why so many are so willing to be deceived. Gullible evolutionists refuse to even question their blind beliefs. This is because it is a moral issue. Darwinian evolution (in the minds of believers) gets rid of the God of the Bible, the issue of sin, and the reality of Hell. The theory of evolution is a very thin bush behind which the atheist thinks he can sin to his heart's delight and not be seen by God.

Man is a deceiver and at the same time he is easily deceived. The essence of deception is that a deceived person will not know he is deceived. This is why we need the Word of an immutable God as a light to our path and a lamp to our feet.

ART EXPERTS

A group of self-appointed art experts stood around a beautiful painting. They admired each brush stoke, with its vibrant colors and its sheer brilliance. It was utterly unique in style. It was a masterpiece.

One of the experts suddenly noticed a very small signature at the bottom of the painting. He leaned forward to take a closer look, stood back, and with utter disdain said the artist's name and used the "n" word to describe him. They hated this man and all of his work, simply because of his skin color. Immediately they took out a small knife and carefully scraped off the artist's name until it was no longer visible.

God knows (and you know) why those who deny God's existence come up with the same arguments over and over. They, as the Bible says, "hate God without cause." They see the expression of His utterly brilliant handiwork. He gave them the gift of life itself and painted the landscape of this world with breathtaking beauty and they scrape any semblance of His name from the canvas. Simply because of His moral government, they disdain the God who gave them life.

And it's clear that the atheists' aggressive agenda is to remove God's name from schools, from currency, from nature programs, and from history books, and at the same time fill movies and television with His name used in blasphemy.

But our concern isn't for God. The Bible says, "God is not mocked. Whatever a man sows, that shall he reap." All they are doing is storing up wrath that will be revealed on the Day of Wrath. They are like a stunted, blind, and crippled flea, shaking his rebellious little fist at a massive herd of ten thousand wild stampeding elephants. They had better move out of the way while they still have time.

CHAPTER EIGHTEEN

BIKERS,
AN ATHEIST,
AND VAMPIRES

I HAD BEEN speaking to a group of pastors and talked for a few moments about the subject of atheism. I told them that one in four professors in colleges and universities was either atheistic or agnostic, and that the number of atheists in the United States had doubled in the last twenty years. Yet it is easy to make a thinking atheist backslide. I had seen it many times, and even have atheists changing their minds instantly on camera. I said that all they had to do was ask an atheist if he believed that nothing created everything. It's like a light goes on in the head of the atheist. He thinks, "Nothing *can't* create a thing. If it *created* something then it's not 'nothing,' it is some sort of creative force." So he is forced to say, "No, I don't believe that." So I give him the only alternative. I say, "So you believe that *something* created everything, but you don't believe it was God?" They usually see that such logic makes sense and say "Yes." So I say, "So you're not an atheist. You believe that there was a creative force, and you just don't know what it is?" to which they agree.

The local pastor planned to take me fishing the next day. It was going to be hot so we called at a store and purchased some shorts and a pair of sneakers. He said that he had spare and unused socks he would give me the next morning. And so he did. They were "ankle" socks. It was early on a Saturday morning and he told me that before we went out for breakfast he had been asked by some Christian bikers to pray for them before they set out on a long ride. He said that there were quite a number of non-Christians that would ride along. As I looked at the bikes and the filthy stickers them and on their Nazi helmets, I could see that he was right. I asked if I could speak to them before they left. We checked with the head honcho, and he said it was okay.

So, what do you say to seventy bikers that look like they could have you for breakfast? I stepped into the middle of them, introduced myself, and said, "You probably realize that I'm not a biker." I was speaking to longhaired, bearded, two-three-hundred pound, tattooed, and leathered tough-looking *hombres*. I was in shorts, one hundred and fifty pounds, white sneakers, and speaking with a weird "down-under" accent. When I told them that the pastor gave me the girlie socks, they laughed. I began by saying, "You may know that there's five times more chance of being killed on a bike than in a car." They gave grunts of agreement. Obviously their experience confirmed the statistic. I then said, "You may not be thinking of Heaven at the moment, but if you have an eighteen-wheeler heading for you at 60 mph and at around ten feet from your face, you may just be thinking of Heaven at that moment. I want to make sure I see you there, so let's go through a few of the Ten Commandments to see if you will make it." I asked if they had lied, stolen, used God's name in vain, or looked at a woman with lust. If they had, they were lying thieves, blasphemers, and, according to Jesus, adulterers at heart, and that if they died in that state, they would end up in Hell. I added, "Some of you may have been to prison, so you will understand the principles of law. God is rich in mercy and sent His Son to suffer and die on the Cross. In doing so, Jesus paid the fine for the Law that we broke. Here's a summary. God is the Judge. You having violated His Law (the Ten Commandments), Jesus paid your fine and rose from the dead; so that means God can legally dismiss your case. He can let you live. All you need to do is repent and trust in Him as your Savior and Lord, and God will give you everlasting life. So make sure you are right with God before you get on your bike today." They listened. No one ate me for breakfast. They weren't offended or angry, probably because what I had said made sense, and they could feel that I simply cared about them and where they would spend eternity.

After breakfast we drove with two other Christians for about an hour until we arrived at a beautiful lake. It was so picturesque that I remember thinking there couldn't be an atheist in the area. I can understand how an atheist could believe what he believes in a rat-infested, crime-ridden, overcrowded, smog-drenched city. But not this place. It had snow-capped mountains, green pastures with tiny vibrant-colored yellow flowers that looked so beautiful it was breathtaking. The lake was a mirror, reflecting the deep blue color of a cloudless sky. We could see bald eagles flying majestically to massive trees, perching and surveying that lake like a king looks over his kingdom. It was an incredible painting and only a fool would dare say that it was painted by nothing.

"You may not be thinking of Heaven at the moment, but if you have an eighteen-wheeler heading for you at 60 mph ten feet from your face, you may just be thinking of Heaven at that moment."

As the men unhooked the boat I walked across to a man who was standing alone about fifty feet from us and handed him a trillion-dollar-bill gospel tract.[1] He laughed, and as I was about to walk away I said, "It's a gospel tract. What your name?" He said it was Milton. I asked "Milton, what do you think happens after somebody dies? Do you think that there is a Heaven?" He said, "I hope so." I said, "Are you good enough to go there?" he said, "Not if God is going to judge me by the Ten Commandments." I was amazed at his answer. He had obviously been thinking about the issue, so we went through some of the Commandments. He was right. Milton would end up in Hell if God gave him justice. I shared the good news of the Gospel with him, told him that he needed to repent and trust the Savior. We then prayed together and hugged, and when I left he had tears in his eyes.[2]

The next day, I was I was about to speak at an important combined church meeting in Klamath Falls, Oregon, when someone said that an atheist had come in and was sitting in the front row, just in front of the pulpit. I say that it was an "important" meeting because it's not often that local churches come together in unity, so we were hoping everything would run smoothly.

I learned he was a university student and that he had recently stood up during a previous church service, disrupted it, and had to be escorted from the church. Apparently he had done it to win a six-pack of beer. The prize was offered by a group of atheists for anyone who would interrupt a church service. I went out to the auditorium, welcomed him, and found out that his name was Abel. I then sat on the platform with the pastor and discreetly eyed Abel as the congregation sang. I couldn't help but wonder what he would say when he interrupted me. I thought that if the atmosphere became tense, as it often does in such circumstances, I could say that his name was Abel, and that when atheists ask me where Cain got his wife I say, "I would tell you if I was Abel."

During the meet-and-greet time I decided offered Abel my bottle of water as a small gesture of love for him. He said that he had his own water and that I would probably need mine during the service (probably because my mouth would go dry when he began yelling at me).

It was then that I noticed a small green book in his hand. It was a Gideon New Testament. When he said, "I'm a big fan of 'The Way of the Master' [television program]," I asked, "Are you a Christian?" He said, "Yes. I became one this morning."

Needless to say there was no interruption, and after the service we both had a great time of fellowship together. How cool.

That afternoon my flight was delayed and I missed my connecting flight from Portland back to Los Angeles. The wonderful thing about being a Christian is that God promises to work everything that happens to us, no matter how bad, for our good (see Romans 8:28). The only way I could get home was to fly farther north to Seattle then back down to L.A. I concluded that perhaps God wanted me to talk to someone on the plane. I found myself sitting next to a 6'5", thirty-one-year-old bartender from Alaska who was reading a novel about vampires. Nick and I talked about Alaska for a while, then I said, "Nick, I have a question for you. What do you think happens when someone dies? Is there an afterlife? He thought that there was, but nothing like Heaven and Hell. I said, "If there was a Heaven, do you think that you are good enough to go there? Are you a good person?" He said that he was, but after going through the Commandments he realized that he wasn't. He was a self-admitted liar, a thief, a blasphemer, an idolater, and an adulterer at heart. He was extremely receptive to the good news of the Gospel and even said, "God bless you" as he left the plane."

When I finally arrived home Sue told me that I missed an earthquake. She was sure pleased to see me. She was upstairs when it shook the house, and it was pretty scary. The next morning she told me that the quake was big enough to shake a basket of ornaments off our TV. Fortunately, they didn't break. I pointed to the straps on the sides of the set that I had wisely connected to the wall to make it stable. And it was stable. A woman needs a man to protect her. I rocked the TV to show her how it would have reacted during the quake. The ornaments fell off and broke.

CONCLUSION

Thank you for taking the time to read this book. May I end with a thought-provoking comment written by a reader of my blog.[3]

> Imagine a scenario where you are suddenly presented with absolute proof that God exists. Not proof that you can reproduce in a lab or record in a scientific journal, but experiential proof that is clear and undeniable...but only to you. I can't tell you what that proof looks like, because it's different for just about everybody. I can tell you what it looked like for me, and I'll do so shortly.
>
> The mind of the Natural man (atheist) will buck against imagining such a thing, and resist even considering the scenario, but I'm asking you to try anyway. Take yourself, with all of your vast scientific knowledge of the universe, and imagine that the Christian God revealed himself to you in an undeniable way.
>
> How would such a thing change your life? What would happen to all the knowledge that seemed to so clearly disprove God just a minute ago? I can tell you exactly what would happen, because it happened to me (minus the vast scientific knowledge part). All that stuff stops mattering.
>
> You begin to realize that what we don't know outweighs what we do know by an astronomical amount. You realize

that What We Know is only an insignificant grain of sand on an unimaginable desert of "Things to Know." You begin to realize that in spite of the fact that we can't agree on what happened throughout eternity, eternity still happened, and something happened inside of it. Lots of somethings. You begin to realize that sometimes both sides of an argument can claim the same piece of evidence. It's all about perspective.

So there you stand. Everything that you once KNEW laying shattered and broken at your feet, and the searchlight of your curiosity that drove you to become so knowledge-able about science and stuff is now focused on the Bible, the one and only source of knowledge about the magnificent creator of the universe. Can you imagine how it feels to suddenly know that such an awesome being actually exists?

Have you ever stood in front of a powerful fan and tried to breath? Every breath you take in fills you up to bursting, and you feel wide open and a little afraid. That's kind of how it feels on the day you start to believe God exists.

It is an awesome day, let me tell you. I've got chills remembering when it happened to me. I was an atheist in an atheist chat room. One day someone came into the room and typed, "imagine a scenario where you are suddenly presented with absolute proof..."

As I imagined, I began to realize that God was POSSIBLE. Afterward, my natural curiosity took the wheel and it was all over for me. God had his revenge, and I became an anti-intellectual (or whatever it is you guys call us these days).

The thing is, I read the posts in this blog, from all of your great minds that have such a clear love for learning, and I get excited because you guys are going to be strong soldiers in God's army when you finally discover the one truth that can change your life. I'll gladly call you my brothers and sisters on that day.

Around 2004, I was with our film crew in Las Vegas. We were interviewing people for our television program outside the famed Bellagio Hotel. One of the reasons it's famous is because it has a magnificent computerized fountain that plays music as water bursts into the sky with each crescendo.

During that time they played some music that almost brought me to tears. I never knew what that song was called, and for years I have longed to hear it again. But recently, to my great joy, I heard it. As I listened to its incredible melody, tears streamed down my face. One of the reasons for the tears was its title. It is called "Time to Say Goodbye." I have often watched people say goodbye to their loved ones at airports and my heart breaks for them, because one day there will be a last goodbye. All of us will say goodbye to everything we love and hold dear to us.

The Christian carries around a deep and heavy sorrow. He is like a man who sees villagers happily living beneath a great dam. He has seen cracks in the dam and he knows that they will soon die if they don't move from where they are living. But the villagers refuse to believe his warning, and even mock his every word. His sorrow is that their deaths will be totally needless.

When I say goodbye to my loved ones for the last time, I will know that I will see them again at the resurrection of the just and the unjust. If you want that incredible consolation, stop doubting and take a long and honest look at the Ten Commandments. They are going to justly damn you forever. Then take a long look at the Savior on the Cross. That's what can save you completely. Then move out of the sinful village of this world, through repentance and faith in Jesus. When your sins are forgiven, instead of having God *against* you, "God will be with you": *Origin of the word Goodbye:* 1565-75; contr. of "God be with ye."

ENDNOTES

PREFACE

1. http://raycomfortfood.blogspot.com/

CHAPTER ONE

1. http://www.edge.org/3rd_culture/turok07/turok07_index.html
2. http://understandingevolution.com/evolibrary/misconceptions_faq.php#a1
3. http://www.answersingenesis.org/articles/nab/did-dinosaurs-turn-into-birds
4. Ibid
5. http://understandingevolution.com/evolibrary/home.php
6. Ibid
7. http://raycomfortfood.blogspot.com/
8. http://www.karger.com/gazette/64/fernald/index.htm
9. Ibid
10. http://www.millerandlevine.com/km/evol/lgd/index.html
11. George Wald, *Scientific American* (1954), http://www.yukoncofc.org/creationvsevolution.pdf
12. http://www.guardian.co.uk/science/2008/feb/09/darwin.dawkins1
13. Ibid
14. Richard Dawkins, *River Out of Eden: A Darwinian View of Life* (New York: Basic Books, 1995), 78.
15. Richard Dawkins, *A Devil's Chaplain* (New York: First Mariner Books, 2004), 212. Italics added.
16. http://raycomfortfood.blogspot.com/
17. http://www.answersingenesis.org/articles/2009/01/13/eyes-have-it
18. http://www.answersingenesis.org/articles/2009/01/13/eyes-have-it#fnList_1_2

19. Richard O. Prum and Alan H. Brush, "Which Came First, the Feather or the Bird?" *Scientific American*, March 2003

CHAPTER TWO

1. http://raycomfortfood.blogspot.com/
2. http://www.huffingtonpost.com/richard-dawkins/why-there-almost-certainl_b_32164.html
3. http://curious.astro.cornell.edu/
4. VIDEO CLIP (see www.PullThePlugOnAtheism.com /):
5. http://discovermagazine.com/2002/apr/cover
6. R.C Sproul, *The Holiness of God* (Carol Stream: Tyndale House, 2000), 10-11.

CHAPTER THREE

1. http://www.newton.dep.anl.gov/askasci/gen99/gen99834.htm
2. http://www.pbs.org/wgbh/nova/origins/knoll.html
3. http://www.time.com/time/magazine/article/0,9171,979365-2,00.html
4. Richard Dawkins (italics added). "Expelled."
5. http://www.newscientist.com/article/dn12506-did-life-begin-on-comets.html
6. http://www.time.com/time/magazine/article/0,9171,979365-3,00.html
7. Ibid
8. http://www.youtube.com/watch?v=zW5-aQonz3E
9. http://www.yale.edu/fes519b/pitchpine/elements.html
10. http://www.buzzle.com/articles/potassium-deficiency-effects-of-low-potassium.html
11. http://www.essortment.com/all/vitaminsmineral_rszw.htm
12. http://www.essortment.com/all/whatismagnesiu_rtca.htm
13. http://www.internethealthlibrary.com/DietandNutrition/Phosphorus.htm
14. http://www.nlm.nih.gov/medlineplus/ency/article/002422.htm
15. http://www.manganese-wilsons-parkinsons-disease.com/
16. http://www.grisda.org/origins/20045.htm

CHAPTER FOUR

1. http://thinkexist.com/quotation/i_want_to_know_how_god_created _this_world-i_am/15496.html
2. http://www.guardian.co.uk/science/2006/apr/06/evolution.fossils
3. Romans 1:18

CHAPTER SIX

1. www2.scholastic.com/
2. www.show.me.uk/site/news
3. http://dinosaurs.about.com/
4. http://dinosaurs.about.com/
5. www.extremescience.com/
6. http://dinosaurs.about.com/
7. *The Expanded Quotable Einstein*, (Princeton: Princeton University), 214.
8. *Albert Einstein*, Brian, op. cit. p. 186.

CHAPTER SEVEN

1. American actor, writer, game show host, documentary filmmaker, conservative political and economic commentator, and attorney. He gained early success as a speechwriter for American presidents Richard Nixon and Gerald Ford.
2. http://curricublog.wordpress.com/2008/11/23/stein-darwinism-gravity-2

CHAPTER EIGHT

1. http://www.lycos.com/info/richard-dawkins—evolution.html
2. http://www.secularhumanism.org/library/fi/dawkins_21_3.html

CHAPTER NINE

1. *The Catholic Encyclopedia*, http://www.newadvent.org/cathen/14783a.htm

CHAPTER TEN

1. Charles Darwin, *Origin of Species*, chapter I. Variation Under Domestication Effects of Habit and the use or disuse of Parts; Correlated Variation; Inheritance.

2. Charles Darwin, *Origin of Species*, page 181.
3. Darwin, C. R. 1871. *The descent of man, and selection in relation to sex* (London: John Murray, Volume 1, 1st edition).
4. talkorigins.org

CHAPTER TWELVE

1. http://www.livescience.com/animals/090211-transitional-fossils.html
2. http://news.sky.com/
3. May 19th, 2009
4. http://www.nypost.com/seven/05192009/news/worldnews/47_million_year_old_fossil_touted_as_mis_170030.htm
5. www.greatapetrust.org/primates/index.php

CHAPTER FOURTEEN

1. http://evolution.berkeley.edu/evolibrary/article/0_0_0/evo_02
2. Ask A Scientist, Biology Archive, http://www.newton.dep.anl.gov/askasci/bio99/bio99927.htm.)
3. www.evolutionary-philosophy.net/sex.html.

CHAPTER FIFTEEN

1. Melanie Phillips, "Is Richard Dawkins still evolving?" *The Spectator*, 23 October 2008.

CHAPTER SEVENTEEN

1. http://www.sanfranciscosentinel.com/?p=27584
2. Carl Sagan, "Cosmos" television series, quoted from "The Carl Sagan Electronic Monument."

CHAPTER EIGHTEEN

1. These are available at www.livingwaters.com
2. I gave Milton two audio messages: "What Hollywood Believes" and "Hell's Best Kept Secret" to encourage him further in his faith.
3. http://raycomfortfood.blogspot.com/